CRIME STRANGE BUT TRUE

Also by James Bland

TRUE CRIME DIARY
TRUE CRIME DIARY VOLUME 2

CRIME
STRANGE BUT TRUE

Some Remarkable Cases

James Bland

Futura

A Futura Book

First published in Great Britain in 1991 by Futura Publications
A Division of Macdonald & Co (Publishers) Ltd
London & Sydney

Typeset by Leaper & Gard Ltd, Bristol
Printed and bound in Great Britain by
BPCC Hazell Books
Aylesbury, Bucks, England
Member of BPCC Ltd.

ISBN 0 7088 4938 5

Futura Publications
A Division of
Macdonald & Co (Publishers) Ltd
165 Great Dover Street
London SE1 4YA
A member of Maxwell Macmillan Publishing Corporation

CONTENTS

CONTENTS

ACKNOWLEDGEMENTS

My thanks are due to Mr Donald Galbraith, Deputy Keeper of the Scottish Record Office, Edinburgh; Miss Suzanne Mourot, former librarian at the Mitchell Library, Sydney, and Mrs Leslie Louviere, Deputy Clerk of Court, St Martin Parish, St Martinville, for information and advice concerning the cases of Margaret Dickson, Joseph Samuel and Willie Francis respectively. I am most grateful for their help.

PREFACE

For *Crime Strange But True* I have written detailed accounts of three dramatic murder cases, all with unusual features but with little else in common. The first concerns the Croydon poisoner Richard Brinkley, a careless man who killed two people unintentionally during an unsuccessful attempt to murder somebody else. This is followed by the famous case of the Lyons Mail murders, an affair involving an apparent miscarriage of justice which was never satisfactorily resolved. And finally, there is one with a curious literary connection: that of 'Snowy' Rowles, an Australian bushman inspired by the plot of one of Arthur Upfield's novels – before it was actually written.

In addition to these three long stories, I have included short accounts of seven other cases under the general title 'Survivors of the Death Penalty'. In each of these, as the title suggests, a capital offender or a person erroneously convicted of a capital offence suffered an abortive execution, all but one of them by hanging. The earliest took place at Tyburn in 1705, the most recent in St Martinville, Louisiana, in 1946. The best known is that of John Lee of Babbacombe, 'the man they could not hang'.

In most of these cases – as in that of Richard Brinkley – only brief accounts are to be found elsewhere, and these are not at all accurate. My own, however, are the result of an extensive search for contemporary sources of information, and therefore contain many facts not previously discovered. I hope that their inclusion will give this book an appeal to those who enjoy the 'stranger than fiction' type of story, as well as true-crime readers in general.

J.B.

THE GENIAL SCHEMER'S
TRAGIC MISTAKE

The Case of Richard Brinkley

1. A sudden and unexpected death

The chain of events leading to the Croydon Poisoning Tragedy, for which Richard Brinkley was responsible, began towards the close of 1906, when the culprit embarked on a fraudulent scheme to acquire the property and savings of an elderly German widow living in Fulham, south-west London.

Brinkley was a middle-aged cabinet maker with a keen interest in poisons. A tall, strong-featured man with a prominent brow, he dyed his grey moustache black, and went about with an air of geniality. His respectable appearance and good humour masked the more sinister side of his nature.

The widow, Mrs Johanna Maria Louisa Blume, was a seventy-seven-year-old retired maternity nurse, generally known by the name of Blombury. She owned a three-storey house at 4 Maxwell Road, where she lived with her granddaughter, Augusta Glanville, an actress aged about twenty-one. She also had savings of £180 in the bank and other money invested in securities.

Brinkley, who was then living in a boarding-house some miles away in Streatham Hill, was on friendly terms with Mrs Blume, and had been visiting her regularly for seven or eight years; he called her 'Granny', gave her advice on business matters, and kissed her each time they parted. So it was not seen as suspicious when, in the latter part of November, he invited her to a social function organized by the local Masonic Lodge, of which he was evidently a member.

Despite her age, Mrs Blume was in good health. She

and Augusta did all their own housework between them and were often seen out in the neighbourhood together. She therefore signed the paper which Brinkley placed in front of her, using her real name at his request. Augusta signed it as well.

It is not clear why Brinkley wanted Mrs Blume's signature on this paper, but obtaining it was the first stage in the scheme which he had devised. He afterwards arranged for a will to be made in her name, making him the sole beneficiary, and either forged her signature on it, as a handwriting expert was later to suggest, or tricked her into signing it herself. The date on this forged will was 17 December 1906.

Augusta Glanville was at this time working at a Fulham theatre, where she had been engaged for the pantomime season. She went off to rehearsals each morning and was often out for much of the day, leaving her grandmother on her own. But on 19 December, not long after Augusta had left the house, the old lady was found dead. The cause of her death was not apparent.

That evening, Brinkley appeared at Maxwell Road himself. He found Augusta, whom he called 'Gussie', talking to a neighbour in the street and was told what had happened. 'Good God!' he exclaimed. He then told Augusta that he had a deed of gift which her grandmother had intended to sign, but made no mention of the will.

Augusta's aunt, Caroline Blume, arrived at the house while they were there together. Caroline, who kept a lodging-house at 68 Alderney Street, Pimlico, assumed that as Mrs Blume's next of kin she was now the owner of the property, and wanted Augusta to leave so that she could take possession of it right away. But at this point Brinkley produced the forged will, claiming that he was now the master there, and showed them the old lady's signature.

They could see no reason to doubt that it was a

genuine document, and Mrs Blume's solicitor, to whom it was shown the following morning, could see no reason to, either.

As Mrs Blume's death had been sudden and unexpected, an inquest was held by Mr S. Ingleby Oddie, who was then the Deputy Coroner for West London. Mr Oddie ordered a post-mortem examination, and this revealed a number of small haemorrhages on the surface of the brain. The doctor, with some hesitation, declared that these were apoplectic in nature and were the cause of death, and the jury, under Mr Oddie's direction, recorded a verdict of natural death from cerebral haemorrhage.

The inquest was held at the Coroner's Court in Fulham on 21 December, and Brinkley was there to observe the proceedings. Mr Oddie, who at this time knew nothing about him, later wrote that he 'must have just glowed with inward satisfaction' when he heard the verdict returned.

2. The tenacious next of kin

Augusta Glanville had not been surprised at the contents of the forged will. She knew that Mrs Blume and Caroline had not been on good terms, and that the old lady had on more than one occasion said that she would leave her daughter nothing. She had also been given cause to expect that she, too, would receive nothing, as a result of her attachment to a young man of whom her grandmother disapproved. Her grandmother 'would get excited when she disagreed with people, and had had fits', Augusta later testified.

Caroline, however, was sure that undue influence had been used to get her mother to sign the will, and instructed her solicitor, Mr J.D. Dutton, to lodge a caveat against it. This meant that it would have to be proved in solemn form, with the two 'attesting witnesses' both swearing that Mrs Blume had signed it in their presence. In the circumstances, they could not do this without committing perjury, and running the risk of being sent to prison.

The first of these 'witnesses' was Henry James Heard, of Camberwell, south London, a little old man who worked as a builder and decorator, though he was actually a carpenter by trade. Heard had visited Mrs Blume in Brinkley's company five days before her death, apparently to repair a damaged ceiling, and the will was in his handwriting. On 31 December – before the caveat had been entered, but perhaps in anticipation of it – he had been prevailed upon to swear an affidavit, stating that he and Reginald Clifford Parker, an accountant (or accountant's clerk) living at 60 Water Lane, Brixton, had been present when the will was signed.

But Parker, a married man with children, could not be relied upon to corroborate this, and was afterwards to claim that his signature on the will had been obtained by trickery. He said that Brinkley had induced him to sign it by pretending that it was an 'outing paper' similar to the one signed by Mrs Blume and Augusta.

Brinkley, at any rate, must have known that Heard's affidavit alone would not be enough to enable him to prove the will in solemn form, and could only hope that it would serve to discourage Caroline from taking the matter to court. When it became clear that it was *not* going to have that effect, he tried to achieve the same end by a different means.

About a month after the funeral – by which time Augusta had left the house in Maxwell Road and he had taken up residence there in her place – Brinkley paid Caroline a visit. He asked her to stop the proceedings, saying that if she would do so he would share the property according to her mother's wishes. But Caroline showed no interest in the offer, and he left without explaining what he had in mind.

Not long afterwards, he went to see her again, and this time asked her to marry him, saying that it had been her mother's wish that they should marry. But Caroline, who did not like Brinkley at all, merely laughed at this idea, saying that she had no intention of settling the dispute *that* way. So he again left disappointed.

In spite of these rebuffs, Brinkley paid Caroline yet another visit, and tried for the third time to get her to 'give up Dutton'. On this occasion, however, she left him in no doubt that she was determined to take the matter to court, and he had finally to accept that these approaches were getting him nowhere. He then decided upon an even more desperate course of action.

3. The intended victim

Besides working as an accountant, Reginald Parker, a clean-shaven, smart-looking man of about thirty-five, ran a fairly large livestock business, dealing in household pets and other animals. He did not manage his affairs well, and during the last quarter of 1906 had debts totalling about £70. He also had matrimonial difficulties of some sort, and he and his wife Ada had already separated twice since their marriage in 1903, and were soon to do so again.

Brinkley, who kept chickens, had got to know Parker well during the year or two preceding Mrs Blume's death; so well, in fact, that at one stage the two men had discussed a scheme to solve Parker's financial problems by means of a fraudulent bankruptcy. Nothing actually came of this idea, but the fact that they discussed it shows that Parker knew the sort of person Brinkley was, and that he was not above breaking the law himself. There was also another aspect of their association.

Brinkley was – in the words of the prosecutor at his trial – 'a bad penman and a bad speller'. To somebody with a propensity to commit fraud this was obviously a disadvantage, but Brinkley managed to overcome it by getting others to do his writing for him. Parker was one of those who occasionally helped him in this way, and it was to him rather than Heard that Brinkley initially turned when he needed somebody to prepare a will in Mrs Blume's name.

Parker later admitted having started to write such a will for Brinkley at his home in Water Lane, but said he thought it was in the name of Johanna Maria Brown. He said that he did not get it finished because Brinkley, who was present, suddenly stopped him after he had written seven or eight lines, saying that his writing was crooked. Brinkley then took it away from him and did not ask him to write it afresh.

The explanation which Parker gave of his signature on the will written by Heard (whom he did not know personally) was rather more complicated. He said that about the time that the unfinished will was written, Brinkley asked him to make out two papers – one a copy of the other – concerning a pleasure outing which he (Brinkley) claimed to be organizing. These were written on ruled paper with cash columns, and comprised nine or ten lines of writing, together with spaces in which the names and addresses of those wishing to go on the outing could be inserted. In this case, there was no complaint about Parker's handwriting.

About three weeks later, Brinkley visited him at Water Lane, and while there asked him to put his own name down for the outing. Parker did so, signing one of the papers and writing his address on it before giving it back to Brinkley.

Afterwards, as Parker was accompanying him part of the way home, Brinkley suddenly asked him to sign the second 'outing paper' as well, saying that he wanted to have a copy that he could keep. He then produced the forged will, carefully folded in such a way that Parker could not see the writing.

Parker was not suspicious. Taking the document into an off-licence which they happened to be passing, in Effra Parade, he asked if he could borrow a pen and ink. It was then after 11p.m., and the lights in the shop were nearly all out. Because of this, he signed the forged will, believing it to be a copy of the paper which he had already signed back at his home.

That, at any rate, was Parker's version of what happened, and the prosecution at Brinkley's trial claimed that he was telling the truth. But, if so, it is hard to see what Brinkley could have hoped to gain from this alleged trickery, for a genuine signature obtained in such a manner would have been of no more use to him than a forged one; he might just as well have written Parker's name and address on the will himself. So if the story was really true, Brinkley must have failed to give sufficient thought to the purpose of what he was doing.

Whatever the truth of the matter, Brinkley knew that if Caroline took her case to court and Parker refused to confirm Heard's sworn statement about the signing of the will, he (Brinkley) would inevitably lose the property which he had gained, and he and Heard would both be in danger of having criminal charges brought against them. He therefore decided that he now had only one course open to him, and that was murder.

4. The undrunk whisky and unfinished tea

By this time, Parker and his wife had parted again by mutual agreement, Parker going into lodgings with his brother in Cobden Road, South Norwood, while Mrs Parker stayed with her parents in Water Lane. Sometime in February, the accountant visited Brinkley at Maxwell Road at Brinkley's invitation and, during the course of this visit, Brinkley, whom he knew to be a teetotaller, offered him some whisky. Parker accepted it, but threw it into the fireplace when Brinkley's back was turned. This was evidently the first of a number of attempts made by Brinkley to poison him.

Some weeks later, on 27 March, Brinkley went to see Parker in Norwood. It was later alleged that he had stolen some prussic acid from a dispenser named William Vale that very day, and that he had taken it to Parker's lodgings with the object of trying again. But he could not do so, as Parker's brother was present.

The following evening, Brinkley called again and found the accountant on his own, writing letters. He offered to make tea while Parker went on with what he was doing, but Parker stopped and made it himself. While they were drinking it, Brinkley asked if he could have some water, so Parker had to leave him in the room on his own while he went down to the scullery to get some for him. On returning, he did not touch his unfinished tea, and so, apparently, survived another attempt on his life.

Nine days after this second visit, Parker left the house in Norwood and went to live at 32 Churchill Road, Croydon, Surrey, the home of a couple named Beck. Richard Beck, aged fifty-five, and his wife Elizabeth, who was two years older, lived there with their two daughters, Daisy and Hilda. They were not in good circumstances, for Richard, a general handyman, was only able to find occasional work. They were therefore forced to take a lodger in an attempt to make ends meet.

Parker settled in with them as best he could, but had for some time been suffering from acute depression. His wife heard about this from Brinkley, who was ostensibly trying to effect a reconciliation between them, and on 13 April went to see him at his new lodgings. She took him to a local doctor who, having examined him, said that her husband was so depressed that he was likely to commit suicide.

Brinkley was told about this by Mrs Parker two days

later. From his point of view, the news could hardly have been unwelcome. But the *possibility* of Parker committing suicide was not enough to prevent his own problem becoming more pressing with each day that passed. It was therefore not long before he made a further attempt on Parker's life: one which had tragic consequences for the other occupants of the house in which the accountant was living.

5. Poisoned by accident

On 18 April, Brinkley wrote to Reginald Parker, whose new address he had been given by Mrs Parker three days previously, asking if he had a dog for sale. He said that he wanted a good house dog and would be willing to pay a good price for it if it was vicious. Parker had such an animal: a white bulldog which a fellow livestock dealer, Thomas Marsh, of Brighton Road, Croydon, was looking after for him. It was arranged over the telephone that Brinkley should see it at Parker's lodgings.

He arrived in Croydon by train on the evening of Saturday, 20 April, with prussic acid in his possession, and before going to Parker's lodgings went into an off-licence in Brighton Road. He had intended to buy a bottle of oatmeal stout, but declined to pay a deposit of 2d on the bottle, and so left without it. However, he returned twenty minutes later, after having second thoughts, and then bought the stout. The dispute about the deposit caused a boy working in the shop to remember him.

When Brinkley reached Churchill Road about 8.20 p.m., Parker and his landlord were drinking beer together in the lodger's private sitting-room, the other members of the Beck family having all gone out. Brinkley took out the bottle of oatmeal stout in their presence, saying that he had been ordered to drink stout by his doctor, and asked if he could borrow a glass. He

11

then drank some of the stout himself and gave some to Parker. He did not pour out the rest of it.

When Beck left them on their own, Brinkley said that he was thirsty and asked if Parker would fetch him a glass of water. Parker went to the scullery to get him one, leaving Brinkley alone in the room. Brinkley thus had an opportunity to put prussic acid into the unfinished bottle of stout without anyone seeing him.

On Parker's return, the two men discussed the bulldog, which was in the room with them. It was agreed that Brinkley would give Parker £5 for it and that the dog would be delivered to his home in Maxwell Road the following morning, as he did not want to take it with him. They then went out for a walk together, parting company about 9.30, when Brinkley caught a tram to Thornton Heath.

Parker took the dog back to Marsh's home, and stayed the night there himself, returning briefly to his lodgings some time after 11 p.m., in order to get a coat. By this time, Elizabeth and Richard Beck and their two daughters, Daisy, aged twenty-one, and Hilda, seventeen, were all indoors; Elizabeth, Daisy and Hilda having arrived home about 10.45, and Richard, who had been out on his own, about fifteen minutes later.

During the time that Parker was there – about ten or fifteen minutes – Elizabeth and Richard were both in the sitting-room, where the poisoned stout stood untouched on the table. After he had left, Daisy went in to join them, Hilda having gone to bed. It was then that the tragedy occurred.

Taking up the bottle of stout, Richard Beck poured what remained of it into two glasses and drank half the contents of one of them himself. His wife took a sip from the other, but said that it tasted bitter and drank no more of it. She and her husband then went out into the kitchen together.

Left on her own in the sitting-room, Daisy drank a

little of the stout herself, but suddenly heard her mother groan and her father call out to her. She tried to go out to them, but before she reached the door she began to feel herself suffocating. She collapsed onto a couch.

Her father managed to rouse Hilda before he, too, succumbed to the poison, but by the time a doctor arrived at the house both he and his wife were dying. They both died within the next few minutes.

Daisy's condition was serious and remained so for several hours. But medical treatment kept her alive and she eventually recovered.

6. Brinkley charged with murder

Shortly after seven o'clock the following morning, Richard Brinkley, unaware that he had committed a double murder a few hours previously, entered a telephone call-box in a newspaper shop in King's Road, Fulham. He rang the number of a shop near Marsh's home in Brighton Road, Croydon, and asked the shop-keeper's daughter, Miss Susan White, to take a message to Marsh for Reginald Parker. He waited on the line while she went to Marsh's house.

Parker had been taken off to Croydon Police Station after being roused from his sleep at 3 a.m., but had asked Marsh to deliver the white bulldog to Brinkley's house. Marsh was getting it ready for the journey when Miss White arrived and told him about the telephone call. He went back to the shop with her to speak to the caller himself.

'I am Brinkley, Fulham,' said the careless poisoner. 'Are you Parker?'

Marsh said that he was not, adding that he was Marsh and that he was going to Fulham. On being asked where Parker was, he replied that he did not know. He had not seen him that morning, he said.

'You tell him not to bring that dog over this morning,'

said Brinkley. 'It will be too ferocious for me. Tell him to come over and see me at six o'clock tonight. If he wants a pound or two he can have it.'

Marsh already knew about the death of Richard and Elizabeth Beck, but did not tell Brinkley about it. He also knew about the bottle of stout which Brinkley – 'a lifelong abstainer' – had taken to their house. He later claimed that it was because of this that he denied knowing Parker's whereabouts that morning.

Brinkley, at any rate, remained in ignorance of his own crimes until many more hours had elapsed. In the meantime, he went to see Mrs Parker, and stayed with her all that evening – hoping, no doubt, that she would soon receive news of her husband's death. But no such news arrived, and he eventually left to return home – only to find two men waiting for him at Maxwell Road.

'We are police officers, and I shall arrest you for administering poison in a bottle of stout to Reginald Parker at Croydon last night, with intent to murder him,' said Detective Inspector Henry Fowler.

Brinkley was taken aback. 'Well, I'm buggered!' he exclaimed.

After being cautioned, he said, 'I was not at Croydon last night.' He was then told that he would probably also be charged with the murder of Mr and Mrs Beck, who had died as a result of the poison. 'Well, I'm buggered!' he said again. 'This is very awkward, isn't it?'

On the way to Fulham Police Station, he said that he had not seen Parker for three weeks. 'I have just left his mother and wife and come from Water Lane,' he said. 'We have been enjoying ourselves.'

Later, as he was being searched, he asked Fowler if he was going to keep him all night. When Fowler said that he was, Brinkley remarked, 'This is Parker playing a trick on me! He is a dirty tyke!'

At about 5 a.m., as he was being conveyed from Fulham to Croydon, he suddenly asked, 'Does Parker say I done it?'

Fowler merely reminded him that he had been cautioned.

'They won't believe him,' Brinkley continued. 'He is a dirty bloody tyke and spiteful towards everyone if they speak to his wife. His mother and wife are beautiful people; they won't have him. I am a good character and a teetotaller. If anyone says I bought beer they have got to prove it!'

Some significance was seen in this remark, as up to that point nobody had said anything to him on the subject of buying beer.

Later, at Croydon Police Station, an identification parade was held, and the boy from the off-licence, John Holden, identified him as the man who, two evenings earlier, had bought oatmeal stout, having first refused to pay a deposit of 2d on the bottle.

By the time he appeared before local magistrates at Croydon Police Court, the fifty-one-year-old prisoner had been charged not only with the attempted murder of Parker, but also with the murder of Richard and Elizabeth Beck and the attempted murder of their daughter Daisy. However, he showed more self-control than before, gazing steadily at the Chairman of the Bench as the witnesses gave evidence against him. It was to be the first of several such appearances.

After hearing the evidence of Reginald Parker, who told the court of the events of Saturday evening, Brinkley asked the witness if he could give the address of the doctor who, the previous week, had said that he should be put under restraint.

'I saw the doctor, but he never mentioned any such thing!' Parker replied indignantly.

At the conclusion of Detective Inspector Fowler's evidence, the prisoner asked whether it was not true that two other people besides John Holden had tried but failed to identify him. Fowler had to admit that that was so.

15

The hearing was then adjourned for seven days, and the prisoner remanded in custody.

7. Mrs Blume's body exhumed

Dr George Genge, the Divisional Police Surgeon, and Dr William Dempster, the local practitioner who had been called to the scene of the tragedy, carried out a post-mortem examination on Tuesday, 23 April, and found – as they had expected to find – that Richard and Elizabeth Beck had both died as a result of prussic acid poisoning.

Fowler, who headed the police investigation, had inquiries made in several districts, and soon learnt of Brinkley's acquaintance with William Vale, a specialist in the diseases of birds.

Vale lived in Manor Road, South Norwood, where he kept his drugs in his private office. Brinkley had twice obtained small amounts of prussic acid from him in June 1906, and had visited his premises on about three subsequent occasions. The last time, in March 1907, he had been left in the office on his own for several minutes, and it was suspected by the investigating officers that he had taken advantage of this opportunity to steal some more of it.

As it was clear from the outset that this was no ordinary murder case, reporters working for the national newspapers watched it unfold with a keen interest. When the story of Mrs Blume's will emerged, a press representative went to see Caroline Blume about it, and Caroline saw no need for reticence on the matter.

She said that she had been much surprised at her mother's sudden death, as her mother had been to see her a few days earlier and seemed quite well then. She also said that Brinkley, to whom her mother had left everything, was 'quite a stranger to us'.

'I was in the house just before the funeral, and

Brinkley ordered me not to touch anything in the place,' she continued.

'About a month after my mother's death, Brinkley came to my house and told me that my mother had said that I owned a house and furniture and earned three hundred pounds by a season's letting. He proposed marriage to me, and said it was my mother's wish that he should marry me, and then we could share the property. I would not have anything to do with him.

'Later, he came again, and said he was about to get work at Victoria Station and must live nearby. He suggested that he should live here, but I told him there was no room.'

When the hearing before the police court was resumed on 29 April, Richard Muir appeared for the prosecution and Walter Frampton for the defence. Mr Muir said that as inquiries were still proceeding he would only call sufficient evidence to justify a further remand.

William Vale and his son both appeared on this occasion, as did Daisy and Hilda Beck. Parker was then called again, and gave evidence at greater length than before. This time he told of his association with Brinkley, and the other attempts which had apparently been made on his life, and again described the events of 20 April.

He said that in November or December previously he had begun preparing a will for the prisoner, from some roughly written instructions, when Brinkley said that his writing was crooked and took the paper away from him. 'The name in the will was Johanna Maria and, I think, Brown,' he declared.

He agreed that his signature on the will produced in court was a genuine one, but said he had not realized that the document was a will when he signed it. He had never met the late Mrs Blume, but had later been to the house in Maxwell Road at Brinkley's invitation. He told the court of the whisky which he was given but did not drink on that occasion, and of the tea which he left

17

unfinished when Brinkley visited him at his lodgings in South Norwood.

After repeating the evidence which he had given before, concerning the evening of the tragedy, he was asked about his matrimonial difficulties, and said that since their marriage in 1903 he and his wife had separated three times by mutual agreement. He also revealed that on Christmas Eve, 1906, he had received a letter signed 'Eva', in which the writer demanded money from him and threatened to lay certain facts before his wife if it was not paid. Parker did not know who was responsible for this letter, and said that he had asked the prisoner if he had caused it to be written. Brinkley had denied it.

At the end of Parker's remarkable testimony, the hearing was again adjourned. Brinkley, who was already haggard and worn after a week in custody, was taken back to Brixton Prison.

The Home Office later issued an order for Mrs Blume's body to be exhumed, as it was now suspected that she, too, had been poisoned.

Mrs Blume had been buried in the same grave as her daughter Augusta – the mother of the young actress – in Brompton Cemetery, a short distance from Maxwell Road. The exhumation of her body took place on Saturday, 4 May, and the examination and analysis were carried out by Sir Thomas Stevenson, the country's leading expert on poisons. But the results of both were unexpectedly negative, so Brinkley could not be charged in connection with the old lady's death.

8. The observant granddaughter

The proceedings before the Croydon magistrates continued for several more weeks, with fresh developments keeping the case in the news. On 6 May Mr Muir told the court of the discovery of certain documents which he said proved that Mrs Blume had been tricked into signing the disputed will in the same way as Parker; these included another paper concerning a social function, this one in Brinkley's own handwriting and unsigned. Five days later, Augusta Glanville, described in one newspaper report as 'a pleasing young lady', was called to give evidence.

Dressed in black, and wearing a large picture hat, she told the court that she and her grandmother had been the only occupants of the house in Maxwell Road, and that Brinkley, whom she had known for seven or eight years, had been a frequent visitor there. She went on to say that in December 1906, while she (the witness) was working at a Fulham theatre, she had been out for the greater part of the day, leaving Mrs Blume in the house on her own.

Replying to questions from Mr Muir, she said that on 14 December, five days before the old lady's death, Brinkley arrived at the house accompanied by Henry Heard, whom the witness had never seen before. They were carrying a bundle of laths, and spoke to Mrs Blume about repairing the ceiling of the top back room, which had been damaged by damp. They went up to look at the ceiling in question, and afterwards left the house, Augusta continued. She could not remember hearing them talk about anything *except* the ceiling.

Two days later, Brinkley called again. This time Mrs Blume was unwell and he was shown into her bedroom, where he remained for three-quarters of an hour. When he came out he expressed concern about the old lady's health, and then, at Augusta's request, went out to buy some milk for them before taking himself off. She did not think that either Brinkley or Heard visited the house the following day, when they claimed that the will was signed.

Augusta also told the court of the occasion when Brinkley spoke to her grandmother about a social outing. 'Will you come, and bring Gussie with you?' he asked her. The old lady replied, 'Yes, I don't mind going.' Brinkley then said, 'Will you sign this paper, then?' Mrs Blume looked at the paper for a long time before answering, but finally said that she would sign it. At his request, she signed it 'Johanna Maria Blume' rather than 'M. Blombury', as she normally signed herself.

Augusta said that when she left the house on the morning of 19 December, her grandmother appeared to be in good health. But not long afterwards she was called from the theatre and returned home to find the old lady dead.

Speaking of the events of that evening, the witness told the court that Caroline wanted to take possession of the house without delay, but Brinkley produced a will, saying that he was now the master there. On being shown the will which bore her grandmother's signature, she agreed that that was the document which he had shown them, adding, 'But these signatures of Heard and Parker, as witnesses, were not on it then.'

After the funeral Brinkley visited the house nearly every day for a fortnight, and then announced his intention of taking up residence there. At this, the witness moved out, but began to visit the house regularly.

Augusta identified a black wig as being similar to one which she had seen in the prisoner's possession. Mr Muir had already suggested that Brinkley's use of such a wig may have been the reason why only one of the witnesses from the off-licence was able to identify him as the man who had bought stout there on the night of the murders.

The witness added that a fortnight after she left Maxwell Road, Brinkley told her that he would divide her grandmother's property between her aunt and herself. The furniture had been intact at that time, but she had since seen part of it in a shop in Chelsea. She had also seen some sheets and other articles which had belonged to her grandmother in a pawnbroker's shop in Brixton Hill.

Cross-examined by Mr Frampton, Augusta agreed that Mrs Blume had more than once said that she would leave nothing to Caroline, and that there had been differences between her grandmother and herself about her young man. She said that the old lady would get excited when she disagreed with somebody, and had actually had fits.

Caroline, a middle-aged woman, was also called. She was rather deaf, and Mr Muir had some difficulty in getting her to understand his questions. She said that on the day of her mother's funeral Brinkley came to tea with her, but declined her request to read the will. She afterwards instructed her solicitor, Mr Dutton, to lodge a caveat against it, and about a month later Brinkley began trying to induce her to discontinue the proceedings. The story about the prisoner's proposal of marriage caused amusement in court, with Brinkley joining in the laughter.

Under cross-examination, Caroline admitted that she had two illegitimate children, and that she had lived with their father – an invalid – for thirty years. However, she denied that her mother had complained about this state of affairs, claiming that for twenty years they had not quarrelled at all.

9. The accountant's wife

On 28 May, after three further adjournments, Richard Brinkley made his final appearance before the Croydon Police Court. He again looked ill, and blinked as the charges were read out to him. The first witness to be called on this occasion was Mrs Ada Parker, the wife of the accountant.

Mrs Parker, a tall, attractive young woman who dressed stylishly, corroborated the statements made earlier about her husband's visit to a Croydon doctor, and said that two days after that visit she told Brinkley

21

that her husband was very depressed and might commit suicide. She identified a card on which she had written Parker's Croydon address and telephone number at the prisoner's request.

On 21 April, the day after the tragedy, Brinkley called at her home in Water Lane, Brixton, and produced a postcard which he had received from her husband, saying, 'How deceitful Reg is to address me as "Dear Dick"!' the witness continued. He did not tell her that he had been to Croydon the previous day.

Cross-examined, Mrs Parker said she knew that Brinkley and her husband had been seeing each other up to the end of 1906. On one occasion her husband told her he had written a will for Brinkley's grandmother, and that Brinkley had said to him, 'Parker, when she dies there's a hundred for you.' He did not say anything about signing the will as a witness.

Mrs Parker was followed into the witness-box by Dr Genge, the Police Surgeon, who said that on arriving at the scene of the tragedy at 3.20 a.m. on 21 April, he found the bodies of Richard and Elizabeth Beck on the kitchen floor and their daughter Daisy in bed. He was shown a stout bottle, which smelt strongly of prussic acid, and had no doubt that prussic acid poisoning had been the cause of both deaths.

Other evidence concerning the cause of death was given by Dr Richard Bodmer, the Public Analyst for Bermondsey, and Sir Thomas Stevenson, whose findings in this case had been positive. The bottle and glasses which had been used by the victims were exhibited in court.

Detective Inspector Fowler was called again, and gave evidence of Brinkley's arrest. He said that at the time the prisoner's moustache had been jet black and curled at the ends, but that after he had washed it, it was grey. He had been allowed to do this before being put up for identification at Croydon Police Station.

The hearing concluded with Brinkley being committed to Guildford Assizes for trial the following month.

10. A hard time for Heard

Two days later, Henry James Heard, one of the 'witnesses' to the forged will, was called to give evidence at the inquest on the two victims. The Coroner, Dr T. Jackson, made it clear from the start that he regarded him with suspicion.

'Now, Mr Heard, this is a very important matter, as you know, and now you are under oath,' he said when the little old man entered the witness box. 'Whatever you may say elsewhere, of course, if you tell us anything contrary to fact, you lay yourself open to a charge of perjury.'

But Heard had already committed perjury, by swearing a false affidavit, and so had either to do so again or make a confession. He chose to do so again, and so told a story which was 'contrary to fact' on many points. He did not give a good impression of himself.

Heard said that he was a carpenter by trade, but now worked as a builder and decorator. He had first met Brinkley about two years previously at the tramway shed in Streatham, where Brinkley was then sub-foreman in the carpenter's shop and Heard worked under him.

Speaking of his visit to Mrs Blume's house on 14 December, the witness said that he went with Brinkley to meet the old lady because Brinkley had said that she wanted him to write a will for her. This was as a result of 'other things' that he had already done for Brinkley.

It turned out that the drafting of the will had already been done, and that she only wanted him to copy it. However, he declined to do it there and then, saying that he would sooner do it at home.

'Did it not seem strange to you that Brinkley was to come in for all the property when there was a granddaughter in the house?' asked the Coroner.

'Yes, it did rather,' replied Heard.

'Did anything else pass between you and Mrs Blume?'

'I said, "I believe you have a daughter?" And she replied, "She is a bad woman. She tried to hit me."'

Heard went on to say that Brinkley told him that a man named Reginald Parker was to be the second witness, and that when he (Heard) took the completed will to the house three days later, Brinkley brought along a man whom he introduced to him by that name.

At this point in the proceedings, the Coroner got Parker to stand up and asked Heard whether he was the man Heard meant.

'Well, I think so,' replied Heard indecisively.

'*Is* that the man?' the Coroner asked again.

'I cannot swear,' said the witness. 'I am under oath, and I am not going to say.'

'*Is that the man?*' demanded Dr Jackson.

Browbeaten thus, the witness suddenly caused astonishment all round by replying, 'I don't think it is, sir!'

Following this sensation, Heard got back to his story. The will, he said, was read aloud, and Mrs Blume then signed it in the presence of the other man and himself. They then signed it as witnesses, and the man introduced as Parker left the house. A fortnight later, Brinkley visited Heard at his workplace in Hornsey, and told him that the old lady had died two days after the will was signed.

'Did not that strike you as a strange, dark coincidence?' asked the Coroner.

'Yes, I remarked that it was very uncomfortable or very awkward that it should have happened so soon,' said the witness.

In reply to further questions, Heard said that Mrs Blume had also asked him to write a deed of gift for her.

'Did you write a deed of gift?' asked Dr Jackson.

'Yes, in pencil,' said Heard.

'Why have you not told the jury anything of that?'

'I have not been asked.'

Questioned by Mr Muir, the witness said that he had copied Mrs Blume's will at Hornsey Road Fire Station, where he was then employed as a watchman. He added that he usually carried a bottle of ink with him, but most likely had not got one on the day of his first visit to Maxwell Road.

When Heard eventually finished giving evidence, after being in the witness-box for nearly five hours, the Coroner said that he did not believe a word of his story, and that it seemed as though he and Brinkley had 'put their heads together'. He would therefore not allow Heard his expenses.

The jury then returned a verdict of wilful murder against Brinkley, who was accordingly committed for trial for the second time in three days – this time in his absence.

11. On trial for his life

Greyer and more anxious-looking than ever, the prisoner was duly placed in the dock at Guildford Assizes on 22 July 1907, to stand trial before Mr Justice Bigham for the murder of Richard Beck. He denied the offence and maintained an air of fortitude as he listened to Richard Muir's opening speech. Even when a thunderstorm broke, and lightning flashed through the courtroom, he continued to gaze at the man presenting the case against him.

Mr Muir spoke for over two hours, and then began calling his witnesses. Daisy Beck and her sister Hilda both described the harrowing events of that fatal evening three months earlier; then Dr William Dempster told of his arrival at the scene while Richard and Elizabeth Beck lay dying. Sir Thomas Stevenson and Dr Richard

Bodmer gave evidence about the cause of these deaths, both having found prussic acid in the bodies of the deceased and the bottle which had contained the stout. Then William Vale, of Manor Road, South Norwood, was called.

Vale told the court that he was a specialist in the diseases of birds, but also treated dogs and cats. He said that Brinkley, whom he had known for fourteen years, had done some carpentry for him in June 1906, and had then asked him for some prussic acid to poison a dog. The witness gave him a small amount of it – about sixty drops – but the prisoner asked for some more a few days later, saying that he had spilt the first lot. He was then given about the same quantity again.

Vale went on to say that he kept his stock of prussic acid in an unlocked cupboard in his office, and thought that Brinkley had seen it there. He also spoke of the occasion in March 1907 when he had left the prisoner in the office on his own for about five minutes. But on being questioned about this by Mr Frampton, he said that he did not think the bottle had been tampered with in his absence.

Vale was followed by Detective Inspector Fowler, who merely repeated the evidence which he had given before the police court. Then Reginald Parker was called to tell his story about the signing of the document which he believed to be an 'outing paper', the incidents of the undrunk whisky and the unfinished tea, and his own part in the events of 20 April. At the conclusion of Mr Muir's examination of this witness the case was adjourned to the following day.

12. Parker's ordeal

Upon its resumption, Parker was cross-examined and soon began to give the impression of being a very unreliable witness. When he was asked how long he had been married, for example, he said that he could not give an exact answer but thought he may have been married in May 1903. In answer to further questions, he said it was true that he had been separated from his wife three times, but he could not remember how long one of those separations had lasted.

'Would you guarantee anything from your memory?' asked Mr Frampton.

'Some things I would!' replied Parker.

But there was worse to come. Asked about his association with Brinkley, the witness said that he had known him for about three years, but had not been on friendly terms with him; only on dealing terms. He had not borrowed money from him, but had given him an IOU for £30 after Brinkley suggested that he should go bankrupt. He did not know whether this was the night that he had done some writing for Brinkley at his home in Water Lane.

'You are an accountant, and he an illiterate man, and you say *he* suggested the fraudulent bankruptcy?' the defence counsel asked him.

'Yes,' answered Parker, though he could hardly have expected to be believed.

'What did he say?'

'That if I gave him that IOU for thirty pounds he would be the biggest creditor, and would get everything carried through for me.'

'And you were prepared to do it?'

'I was.'

The witness went on to admit that as a result of advertisements which he had placed in publications called *Feathered World* and *Cage Birds*, he had received complaints from customers about his dealing methods, and even 'suggestions' of dishonesty.

Questioned about the events of 19 December – the night on which he claimed that Brinkley had tricked him – Parker said that the signing of the document took place at Hennessy's off-licence in Effra Parade, Brixton, about forty yards from his home in Water Lane. He told Mr Frampton that it was just before they reached Hennessy's that the prisoner asked him to sign it, pretending that it was just a duplicate of the 'outing paper' which he had already signed back at the house.

'Did he give you the paper to look at?' asked Mr Frampton.

'Yes,' said the witness.

'And you went into Hennessy's shop to sign it?'

'Yes.'

'Brinkley remaining outside?'

'At the door.'

'You had to ask for a pen and ink?'

'Yes.'

'Did you look at the paper?'

'No.'

'What? Did you write your name and address without looking at it?'

'Certainly – oh, no! Not without looking at it.'

'Did you see whether it was the same paper which you had written?'

'No, I took it that it was.'

'The signature on this will is yours?'

'Yes.'

'There are no money columns on the paper?'

'No.'

At this point the judge read Heard's affidavit, stating that the two witnesses had signed the will in Mrs Blume's presence. Mr Frampton then resumed his cross-examination of the witness.

'Now, I put it to you that it would be impossible for you to sign that paper in Hennessy's house without knowing that those money columns were not there,' he said.

'The light was bad,' replied Parker.

'The night you signed the IOU, did Brinkley ask you to go and witness a will for him?'

28

'No, he never asked me to witness a will in his life.'

'Did you go to Maxwell Road one day in your dinner hour and sign the will in Mrs Blume's presence?'

'No.'

'Have you told your wife that you witnessed a will for Brinkley?'

'Never.'

'And that it was Brinkley's grandmother's will?'

'No, sir.'

'And also that when the old lady died you would get a hundred pounds?'

'No, sir.'

Replying to further questions, Parker said that he had not suspected Brinkley of trying to poison him. He had accepted the whisky offered to him at Maxwell Road in February because he did not want to refuse the prisoner's hospitality, but did not drink it because whisky always upset him. As for the cup of tea left unfinished at his lodgings in Cobden Road, he said that he did not drink that because it had got cold by the time he returned from the scullery.

Asked whether he had passed himself off as a single man when he went to stay with the Beck family, Parker admitted that he had. He had to agree that when his wife visited him there, on 13 April, he had introduced her to the Becks as his young lady, and that he later told Dr Everington – the doctor who said he was likely to commit suicide – that she was his sister.

So, by the time his two-hour ordeal was over, Parker's story had been shown to be even more incredible than it had seemed before, and there must have been some present who wondered whether it could really be given any credence at all.

13. Scientific evidence

When Mrs Parker gave evidence a little later – after a

29

brief appearance by Dr Everington – she told the court of an incident which had occurred during one of the prisoner's visits to Water Lane. She said Brinkley and her husband were in the sitting-room together, and her husband was writing. But when she (the witness) entered, Brinkley suddenly took the paper away from him.

Under cross-examination, Mrs Parker also repeated the claim which her husband had denied. Asked whether she had once complained because Parker came home late, she replied, 'Yes, and he then said that he had been writing a will.'

'For whom?'

'For Brinkley's grandmother. My husband said that Brinkley had told him that when she died he would have a hundred pounds.'

After Mrs Parker, several witnesses gave evidence concerning the events of 20 April and the following morning. These included Henry Daw, an inspector on the West London Extension Railway, who said that he had seen Brinkley at Chelsea Station about 6 p.m. on 20 April, and John Holden, the boy from the Croydon off-licence where Brinkley had bought the bottle of stout.

Augusta Glanville was unable to appear personally, as she was ill with scarlet fever, so her deposition was read by the Clerk of Arraigns. Caroline Blume then gave evidence to the same effect as before, followed by her daughter, Caroline Eugenie Blume, who said Brinkley had told her that if her mother would only give up her solicitor they could all share her grandmother's property.

Further evidence for the prosecution was given by Mr T.H. Gurrin, a handwriting expert, and Mr C. Ainsworth Mitchell, a Fellow of the Institute of Chemists. Mr Gurrin said that Mrs Blume's signature on the disputed will bore none of the characteristics of her handwriting and many of the characteristics of the prisoner's own handwriting – which was hardly consistent with the allegation that she had been tricked into signing it – and

Mr Mitchell said that he had examined the ink on the document microscopically and found that three different types had been used. Heard's signature was in the same ink as that used in the body of the will, Mrs Blume's was in a different one, and Parker's was in the same ink as that used at the off-licence in Effra Parade.

It was the first time that evidence of ink analysis was given in a court in this country.

When Mr Mitchell left the witness-box, the case for the prosecution closed and the court adjourned again.

14. Transparent mendacity

On the third day of the trial, Brinkley gave evidence on his own behalf, remaining in the witness box for over six hours. Observed by an even larger gathering of spectators than had been present during the previous two days, he denied the allegations that had been made against him, and shed tears freely when that seemed the appropriate thing to do.

Brinkley told the court that he had known Mrs Blume – or 'Granny' as she was referred to throughout his evidence – for twenty-two or twenty-three years, and was on very friendly terms with her. She spoke to him several times about making a will, and he agreed to get somebody who could do it for her. It was for this reason that he introduced her to Henry Heard a few days before her death.

In reply to questions about what had happened on that occasion – the visit of 14 December – he said that Augusta was in the house when he and his companion arrived, and that Mrs Blume asked them to pretend that they had come about the damaged ceiling. So, having been up to look at the ceiling in question, they left the house together and did not return until an hour and a half or two hours later – by which time Augusta had gone out.

Heard then went into the breakfast parlour with the old lady while the witness went upstairs with some wood laths. A few minutes later, the two men left the house together, after arranging to call again the following Monday.

Asked why they were to go back there on the Monday, Brinkley said that Heard had told him that he had been given instructions concerning Mrs Blume's will. He did not tell the witness what those instructions were.

'Have you ever told this story to anybody before?' asked the judge.

'No,' admitted Brinkley.

'Not to a solicitor?'

'No, my lord.'

'Why not?'

'I have never been asked.'

Continuing his evidence, Brinkley said that one night between 14 and 17 December he called on Parker and his wife at their home in Water Lane, Brixton, and asked the accountant if he would witness a will for him. Parker said that he would, and asked Brinkley if he would mind accepting an IOU from him for £30, as he was being pressed by his biggest creditor. Brinkley agreed to this, and gave Parker the money in exchange for the document. Before parting company that night, they agreed to meet at Mrs Blume's house on the Monday.

Brinkley denied that he had ever got Parker to write a will for him, and said that he had never asked him to sign an 'outing paper'. He had once shown him a paper concerning a Masonic function, but had not got him to put his name on it.

'Did you ever ask Parker in the street to put his name to any form?' asked the defence counsel.

'Never,' said Brinkley.

The prisoner went on to say that he met Heard near Chelsea Station between ten and eleven o'clock on the morning of 17 December, and that they went for a stroll together, arriving at Maxwell Road soon after one o'clock. Parker met them there, as arranged, and the three men went into the back parlour with Mrs Blume. But Brinkley then left the room, to let the old lady's dog out into the garden, and so was not present when the will was signed and witnessed.

Parker left the house a few minutes later, and Brinkley and Heard followed. But Brinkley returned on his own shortly afterwards, and was then given the completed will, Mrs Blume warning him that 'if they get hold of it they will destroy it.' He did not see her alive again.

Asked about the events of Wednesday, 19 December, the prisoner said that he arrived at Maxwell Road about eight or nine o'clock in the evening and saw Augusta talking to a neighbour out in the street. Augusta told him that her grandmother was dead, and he then said that the old lady had been preparing a deed of gift which she was going to sign. He suggested that they should look for it.

By this time, Caroline Blume was already at the house; she had taken charge of the keys and wanted to turn Augusta out there and then. Brinkley told her that he had her mother's will, and took it out of his pocket to show her; he then asked her to give up the keys, and she threw them onto the floor. Brinkley remained at the house for about two hours before returning to Streatham Hill, where he was then living.

When he was asked about the subsequent occasions on which he had seen Caroline, the prisoner admitted that he had visited her three times after hearing about the caveat on 9 January, but said that he had not tried to persuade her to stop the proceedings and had not proposed marriage to her.

Replying to a question about one of his visits to Parker's lodgings in Norwood, he said that Parker had wanted him to go over and see the place. The first time he went there he offered to go again the following day and prepare Parker's tea for him, but Parker declined the offer. Brinkley nonetheless went to see him the next day, arriving about tea time.

'Is it true that you drank up a cup of tea, and then asked Parker to fetch you a glass of water?' asked Mr Frampton.

'Oh, no!' said Brinkley. 'It was a long time after that.'

He claimed that he had been on friendly terms with Parker up to that time. There had been no differences whatever between them, and he (the witness) had been trying to bring Parker and his wife back together, he said.

Brinkley went on to admit that he had obtained prussic acid from William Vale on two occasions in June 1906, saying that he had wanted it to poison a dog which was worrying his fowls, and had used it all for that purpose. He also agreed that the following March, when he went to Mr Vale for some pills, he was left in his office alone for some minutes. However, he denied touching the prussic acid in the dispenser's absence, and said that he had no poison in his possession when he went to see Parker later the same day.

In answer to further questions from Mr Frampton, Brinkley claimed that he had never been to Churchill Road, Croydon, and had never been to the off-licence where he was alleged to have bought the stout. He said that his bargain with Parker concerning the white bulldog had been made over the telephone on the morning before the tragedy, when it was agreed between them that Parker should bring the dog over to Fulham for him the following day. The prisoner spent part of that Saturday evening in the company of Mr Snapper, a shopkeeper of King's Road, Chelsea, then went home and fell asleep.

The next day he changed his mind about the dog, and tried to send Parker a message by telephoning the shop near Marsh's home. He said he thought the animal was too ferocious for him.

At this point the examination of the prisoner ended

and the court adjourned for lunch. When it resumed, Mr Muir began his cross-examination by challenging Brinkley's account of his movements on the evening of 20 April.

'Can you tell us the name of a single living person who saw you on the night of the murder, between six and nine?' he asked.

'Yes,' said Brinkley. 'Mr Snapper.'

'Is Mr Snapper here?'

Brinkley glanced round the court and said that he could not see him.

'If he can prove what you say, why is he not here?'

The prisoner's failure to reply showed clearly that he did not have the alibi which he had pretended to have.

Brinkley also had to admit that the inspector at Chelsea Railway Station, who said that he had seen him that evening, was somebody he had known for years.

However, he continued to deny that he had been to Croydon on 20 April, and said he could not say why Parker had claimed that he *was* there.

Questioned about the probate suit, he said that he had heard from his solicitor on 16 April that the defence had been delivered, and had an appointment to go to his solicitor's office the following day. The day after that (18 April), he wrote to Parker about the dog.

There were further questions about the prisoner's last visit to William Vale, even though Vale himself had said that he did not think his bottle of prussic acid had been touched in his absence. Mr Muir then went on to establish that Brinkley's interest in poisons was greater than the earlier evidence had suggested.

'You admit having asked Mr Vale for prussic acid last year?' he asked.

'Yes,' said Brinkley.

'Did you yourself buy Shield's prussic acid some years ago?'

'I bought some, but don't know whose it was.'

35

'So that for years you have known prussic acid?'

The prisoner did not answer.

When Brinkley denied having made a study of poisons, Mr Muir produced a piece of paper which had been found at Maxwell Road, containing the information that nitrate of silver could be detected in ordinary water but not in distilled water. Asked why that had been in his possession, the prisoner replied, 'I was in the habit of buying distilled water and I told Mr Vale so; and Mr Vale asked me if I knew whether I was getting it, and he gave me the test. That was two or three years ago.'

He said that he knew nitrate of silver was a poison and had never tried the test.

Questions concerning Mrs Blume's will followed, and finally Mr Muir came to the subject of the 'outing paper' which the old lady had been asked to sign.

'Beyond getting her signature into your possession, can you give the jury any reason why you got the old lady to sign this document?' asked Mr Muir.

'No,' replied Brinkley.

'Be careful!' said the judge. 'Think of the significance of your answer.'

It was not the first time he had been cautioned in this way: in fact, Mr Justice Bigham had several times warned him to weigh and consider his words. But Brinkley could only repeat the answer that he had given before, adding that he may have wanted to send the lists of names to his Lodge.

He was then shown another paper which had been found in his possession. It was in his own handwriting and contained the words, 'I hereby declare myself a visitor of Mr Richard Brinkley's to the annual ladies' ball; also my niece, Augusta Glanville.' Asked what these words meant, he said that he did not know. He did not recollect anything about them, and could not say whether he had intended to get the old lady to sign the document.

And so this display of what one observer called 'transparent mendacity' drew to a close, and Brinkley returned to the dock. Nobody else was called on his behalf; not even Henry Heard. So, after Thomas Marsh had been recalled to answer a question from the judge, the court adjourned to the next day.

By this time, the ground gained by the defence in discrediting the prosecution's chief witness had been irretrievably lost.

15. No Heard, no Snapper

When the judge took his seat on the morning of the fourth day, Richard Muir rose and began his final speech for the prosecution. He told the jury that they had two questions on which to base their verdict. One was whether Brinkley had any motive to murder Reginald Parker; the other was whether Brinkley was in Croydon on the night of 20 April. He said that if the answer to both was in the affirmative, as the prosecution contended, then a verdict of guilty must follow.

He then went on to deal with the question of motive, saying that if Mrs Blume's will had been put forward by Brinkley with the assertion that Parker's name had been put on it as a witness in Mrs Blume's presence, and that was proved not to be the case, then a motive for Parker's murder existed. As proof that that was what had happened, he cited the discovery of three different types of ink on the document; a fact which Brinkley had tried to explain by saying that there had been three bottles of ink in the house at the time the will was made.

'Seek for corroboration of any important statement of Brinkley's and you will find none!' declared the prosecutor.

At this point, he reminded the jury that Heard and Parker, according to Brinkley, had both signed the will in Mrs Blume's presence.

'Where is Heard?' he asked. 'Why is Heard not called, if that is a true story?'

On the evidence, it was impossible to consider the will a genuine document, and if it was a forgery, then it was quite impossible for Reginald Parker to have put his name to it in the presence of Mrs Blume, the speaker continued.

Turning to the question of whether Brinkley had been in Croydon on the night of the murder, Mr Muir said that the man who *was* there took a bottle of oatmeal stout and put prussic acid into it, intending it for Parker. Who, had it been shown to the jury's satisfaction, knew about prussic acid? he asked. Who used prussic acid, who had prussic acid in his possession, and who had access to prussic acid just about this time?

'Brinkley!' he said, in answer to his own question.

Brinkley had said that he hadn't been to Croydon that Saturday night, but stayed at the house of Mr Snapper until seven o'clock, the prosecutor pointed out. Mr Daw, the Inspector at Chelsea Station, contradicted that, but he in turn could be contradicted by Snapper, if the prisoner's story were true.

Where was Snapper? asked Mr Muir. How was it that a valuable witness, who could corroborate Brinkley's story, had not been placed in the witness-box? There could be only one reason, and that was that if Snapper *were* called he would not corroborate the prisoner's story.

'My submission to you is that evidence for the Crown has established a motive on the part of Brinkley to murder Parker, and evidence for the Crown has established that Brinkley was in Croydon on the night of 20 April; that he brought that bottle of stout into Parker's room, and put prussic acid into it with the intention that Parker should drink it,' concluded Mr Muir. 'If that is so, then the verdict must be for the Crown.'

When Mr Muir sat down, Mr Frampton rose to

address the jury on the prisoner's behalf. He said that of all the forty witnesses called by the prosecution only three had dealt with facts, and they were Parker, Holden and Daw. The allegation of the forged will was a prejudice imported into the case, for no plea of forgery had been put on the record in the probate action, he continued.

Mr Frampton cited the evidence of Augusta Glanville in support of his contention that Mrs Blume had intended to make a will in Brinkley's favour, and brushed aside the evidence of Mr Gurrin, the handwriting expert, by reminding the jury that Augusta had identified her grandmother's signature as a genuine one. He also said that Brinkley's story was corroborated by the evidence of Mrs Parker, who said her husband had told her that he had prepared a will for the prisoner and was to have £100 for doing so.

Speaking of Parker, upon whose testimony the Crown had asked the jury to rely, Mr Frampton pointed out that he was a man who had contemplated a fraudulent bankruptcy. When he signed the will for Brinkley in the Brixton off-licence, believing it to be an 'outing paper', he failed to notice that it had no cash columns, even though he had signed an 'outing paper' *with* cash columns a few minutes earlier. And although he did not care where he put his name, he yet, by some curious accident, wrote it at the foot of the document, beneath some other signature, observed the defence counsel.

Coming to the events of 20 April, Mr Frampton said that with the exception of Parker, Daw and Holden were the only witnesses who said that they had seen the prisoner that day. He asked whether it was not remarkable that the inspector should remember having seen Brinkley at Chelsea Station that evening when there was no record of any ticket for Croydon having been bought there. As for Holden, he was only one of three people who had been in the shop in Brighton Road when the bottle of stout was bought, but neither of the others had been able to identify the accused. Surely a mistake had been made?

Mr Frampton described Parker's account of that evening's events as an unlikely one. The prisoner was said to have gone to a house which he did not know, and where he did not know how many people he would meet, and when he arrived there he produced from his pocket a bottle of stout, into which he put poison, then left the house with Parker. Was that a probable story? the speaker asked.

Mr Frampton concluded his address by saying that there were many strange and unexplained features in the case. To him, Parker was an enigma, and he did not know why he had told one story to his wife and another to the court. Yet Parker was the prosecution's chief witness. Unless the jury accepted his evidence, they could not convict the accused. On the other hand, they could not convict *on* his evidence. The only verdict they could reach was therefore one of acquittal.

Mr Justice Bigham, in his summing-up, said that the jury had to decide whether the prisoner had taken poison to the Becks' house on 20 April, with the intention of poisoning Reginald Parker. If he had done so, and while trying to poison Parker had unintentionally poisoned somebody else, then he was guilty of murder, the judge explained. But in order to decide that, the jury would have to consider other questions, including that of whether Brinkley had had any motive for trying to poison Parker.

They would probably be of the opinion that Mrs Blume had had an affection for Brinkley and wanted to benefit him in some way, but that would be of no use unless it was carried out by a will or a deed of gift. About a month before her death the prisoner visited the old lady frequently, and in November or at the beginning of December he procured her to sign an 'outing paper', using her real name, Johanna Maria Blume, though she was generally known by the name of Blombury. He was unable to give any reason for asking her to sign her name in that way.

There was evidence that an attempt had been made by Parker to write out a form of will, and Mrs Parker said that her husband had told her he was writing a will for Brinkley and was to be paid £100 for it. It was also known that Heard had drafted a deed of gift. On 14 December, Heard, who was a stranger to Mrs Blume, went to her house with Brinkley, and it was said that the old lady then gave him instructions as to her will. On 17 December, Heard returned to the house with Brinkley, taking the will, and Brinkley said that it was then signed in the presence of Heard and Parker. But Parker denied that he had been there at all, or that he ever signed the document as a witness to a will.

That, said the judge, was an issue between the Crown and the prisoner, and there was an easy way of settling it. The jury would ask themselves why Brinkley had not called his friend Heard, who was at the courthouse and could have been called to prove the prisoner's story, if it were true. Mr Frampton, in what the judge called his 'admirable address', had left them in the dark as to why he had not been called.

Reviewing Parker's evidence, and that of Mr Gurrin, the handwriting expert, the judge said that if the will was a forgery, that would form a motive for Brinkley to want to get rid of Parker. The question of whether he had taken prussic acid from Vale's office on 27 March, as the Crown alleged, did not seem very important, as Brinkley had had prussic acid previously and probably knew where to get it. As for his going to Parker's home the next day and asking for a glass of water, that by itself was of no consequence whatever; its significance was derived from its similarity to what was said to have happened at the Becks' house.

After dealing with other aspects of the case, including the proceedings before the Probate Court, the judge came to the events of 20 April. Pointing out that Parker had brought the white bulldog to his lodgings that evening, he asked why that was done if, as Brinkley said, it had already been arranged for the dog to be taken to Fulham the following morning. He then turned to the prisoner's claim that he had an alibi for the early part of the evening and, like Mr Muir, asked why Snapper had not been called as a witness. It was of the highest importance to Brinkley that Snapper should be called, and yet he was *not* called, said the judge.

Finally, he dealt with the evidence of Daw and Holden, saying that if the latter's story was true there could be little doubt that Brinkley was the man who took the bottle of oatmeal stout to the Becks' home on the evening in question.

The jury retired at 2.20 p.m., and returned fifty-five minutes later with a verdict of guilty. Brinkley was then asked whether he had anything to say before sentence of death was passed on him. He shook his head, answering faintly, 'I am not guilty.'

The black cap was placed on the judge's head and the sentence pronounced in its usual form, Mr Justice Bigham making no further comment on the case. Visibly shaken by the verdict, the prisoner stood listening, with his arms folded in a desperate show of resolution. Then he turned and walked down the steps from the dock, his hands twitching convulsively as he disappeared from view.

16. Suicide, fire and poisoned chickens

The prosecution had also had a witness who was not called. He was Sergeant Overton, the Coroner's Officer at Westminster, whose evidence concerned the suicide of a seventeen-year-old Warwickshire girl at a house in

Moulberg Square, Chelsea, fourteen years earlier. The girl, Laura Jane Glenn, had left her home in the mining district of Granton in October 1892, and at the time of her death was living with Brinkley as his wife. She died from the effects of arsenic poisoning.

Brinkley, then known as William Ridgley, was the son of a Lincolnshire farm labourer. Born in 1855, he had settled in London in his youth and married the daughter of a coachman in 1875. His wife, Clara Emily Brinkley, had borne him several children before her death in 1883, but only the eldest of these – his son Richard – appears to have been with him at the time of his affair with Jane Glenn.

At the inquest which followed the girl's death, Brinkley denied that she had slept in the same room as him, in spite of evidence to the contrary. He said that he had taken her to stay at his lodgings after finding her poor and homeless, but soon fell in love with her and wanted her to marry him. He accounted for bottles of arsenic, prussic acid, strychnine and chloroform which had been found in his possession by saying that he used them for 'experimental purposes'. He had carried out experiments in connection with electric light and bells, and had also tried to compete for a £2000 prize which was then being offered for the invention of colour photography, he said.

Brinkley's evidence did not impress the coroner, and although statements the dead girl had made, together with a suicide note which she had left, were enough to clear him of any suspicion of murder, he was criticized for giving false evidence. The Coroner said Brinkley had asked them to believe that he was a man of extraordinary virtue, but as far as they had been able to test his story, they could not place any reliance on it. The jury, in recording a verdict of suicide, added that he was deserving of severe censure for having such a quantity of poison in his possession, and expressed the hope that the police would make every endeavour to find out how and for what purpose he had acquired it.

The evidence concerning Jane Glenn's death was kept in readiness at Guildford, in case Brinkley denied having any knowledge of poison, but as he made no such denial it was not produced. The story was nonetheless published when the trial ended, showing clearly that Brinkley's interest in poisons was of long standing. It was also revealed that Brinkley had been given a prison sentence for stealing a bicycle and other articles about the same time.

From another story about Brinkley – one which emerged shortly after he was arrested in connection with the Croydon murders – it would seem that his pre-occupation during the previous few months with the problem posed by Caroline Blume had not prevented his devising other schemes to make money at the expense of other people.

In an interview with a press representative, Miss Margaret Emma Wade, his Streatham Hill landlady, said that while living at her boarding-house, Brinkley had kept chickens, some of which died after he had given them drugs. Later, after taking up residence at Fulham, he had kept his room on, but had finally been told to leave after causing a fire there.

'On Friday, 15 March, he came over to me and said, "I am bringing some furniture in here from Maxwell Road," but instead of that he moved some out on that day,' continued Miss Wade. 'On the next evening he told me he was going to light a fire in his room, and he went out to get some coals.

'He had never had a fire in his room before, and I told him to be careful, as he had a lot of shavings and paper in the place. I asked him if he was going to sleep here that night, and he said "Yes, I am."

'He was in and out several times during the evening, and after I went to bed I heard him go out at half-past eleven, but did not hear him return.

'At about one o'clock in the morning one of my lodgers, Mr Parks, who is employed on the trams, came in and heard a crash. On going to see what it was, he saw smoke issuing from under Brinkley's door. It was locked, and, as Mr Parks could get no reply to his knocks, he burst open the door and found that the room was on fire.

'There were eight people in the house at the time – most of them asleep – and if it had not been for Mr Parks coming home late, we might have all been burnt to death in our beds.

'When I was called, and found the room on fire, I thought Brinkley had been burnt, but it turned out afterwards that he did not return after I heard him go out. He had insured the contents of his room for two hundred pounds, and I think the insurance company paid thirteen pounds to him.'

Miss Wade concluded her statement by telling the reporter that Brinkley had had a large chest full of drugs and chemicals in his room, and that he had once offered Mrs Parks a mixture for a cold, which Mrs Parks had refused.

Miss Wade's story about the fire may or may not have been true: it was never proved either way. That Brinkley had poisoned chickens, however, was certainly true, for he admitted this at his trial.

17. Justice takes its course

During his nineteen days under sentence of death in Wandsworth Prison, the 'Croydon Poisoner' was quiet and subdued. He gave no trouble to prison officials, and for much of the time occupied himself with reading. He continued to maintain that he was innocent, and expressed the hope that a petition for his reprieve would be successful. He ought never to have been found guilty on such flimsy evidence, he declared. But the petition was not successful, and justice was left to take its course on the morning of 13 August 1907.

Brinkley made it clear that he did not want any visits from his children. Speaking of his son, he said, 'I have not seen him for three years, and I shall not do so now.' When the day of his execution arrived, he rose at 6 a.m., after a restless night. He put on his own clothes in place of the prison clothes which he had worn since his conviction, but was very haggard and could not eat his breakfast.

As the end drew near, he wrote a final letter to his solicitor, Harry Wilson, again insisting that false evidence had been given against him, and this time alluding to some papers 'concerning Fowler and Parker's schooldays together, and their friendship ever since', which he asked Mr Wilson to publish. He went on to declare that he had 'lived a righteous and a sober life', so that 'if it's God's will I am prepared to meat Him at any time and know I am innocent of these poor peoples deth'.

In his will, a typewritten document of about 350 words, he left all his real and personal estate, after the payment of his debts and expenses, to the Royal Masonic Institution for Girls – apart from his Masonic regalia, which he gave to Mr Frampton as a memento 'for the able manner in which he defended me on my recent trial'. His last request was that his watch and chain, and some other articles, should be given to Mr Wilson, whom he had appointed his sole executor and trustee.

A few minutes before 8 a.m., Henry Pierrepoint, the hangman, entered the cell, accompanied by John Ellis, his assistant on this occasion. The Deputy Governor of the prison, the Deputy Medical Officer and the Under-Sheriff of Surrey also entered, and in their presence the prisoner was seized and his arms pinioned without difficulty. Despite the circuitous route to the scaffold, Brinkley managed to remain calm, and had little need for assistance. He continued to bear up, apparently with a great effort, as Pierrepoint (the father of the more famous Albert Pierrepoint) placed the noose round his neck.

'His last words were spoken very distinctly just as I was about to pull the lever,' Pierrepoint later recorded. '"Lord receive my soul," he murmured, and next second, with a drop of 6 ft 8 in, he went down to instantaneous death.'

The usual printed notice was afterwards posted at the main entrance to the prison, informing the crowds outside that Brinkley's sentence had been 'duly carried out according to law'.

Later that month, when details of Brinkley's will were published, the general management committee of the Royal Masonic Institution for Girls resolved 'that his executor ... be informed that the institution declines in any way to benefit under the said will'. But this was not a great sacrifice on the institution's part, for the property left by Mrs Blume was not involved, and Brinkley's estate had been valued for probate at just £10.

The old lady's estate, valued at just over £725 gross (£667 net), eventually passed to her inexorable daughter.

18. A more plausible explanation

In his memoirs, published many years later, Ingleby Oddie, the Coroner, included a chapter about Brinkley, whom he described as 'a jobbing carpenter with a curiously twisted mind and a certain amount of low cunning by which, under a veil of geniality, he sought to perpetrate the grossest crimes, including murder'. He had no doubt that the disputed will was a forgery, or that Brinkley unintentionally poisoned the Becks in an attempt to poison Reginald Parker. He even suspected that Brinkley had murdered Mrs Blume in the same way.

'Brinkley, I realized afterwards, might well have called to see "Granny" after the granddaughter had left the house at ten that morning, and might have induced her to share a bottle of beer with him,' he wrote.

Then he might so easily have added prussic acid to her glass in her absence when he had (perchance) asked her to go and get him something, such as a glass of water. In view of what happened later, I have often thought this was exactly what he did.

I know of no poison which causes death so quickly – in an hour – except prussic acid and its derivative, cyanide of potassium. This poison kills in a few minutes; others will take many hours. Prussic acid, taken in solution on an empty stomach, often kills in a few seconds, like a fatal stroke of lightning and in exactly the same way, that is by paralysis of the breathing.

Hence a sudden spasm caused by prussic acid immediately preceding death might well have produced the small punctate haemorrhages found in Mrs Blume's brain. At the same time, whilst it is true that it is almost impossible to miss the detection of this poison at the post-mortem examination and even before opening the body – owing to the terribly pungent smell of bitter almonds which pervades the whole of the organs – yet I have known doctors who could never smell it at all.

One of my very best pathologists was quite unable to detect the smell of cyanide, even when it filled the whole room with suffocating pungency to the noses of other people, and it may well be that, if there was cyanide in Mrs Blume's body, it was missed in this way at the post-mortem examination. Apart from the odour, it leaves no very marked and characteristic signs in the organs perceptible to the naked eye which would enable a pathologist to detect it if he did not notice the characteristic smell.

Explaining that the negative results of Sir Thomas Stevenson's examination and analysis of the body five months later could have been due to the volatility of the poison, Mr Oddie concluded: 'I cannot, even now, help feeling that Brinkley had something to do with the old lady's death in view of the suddenness with which it took place after her granddaughter left the house, and the date of the completion of the will only two days before.'

This 'feeling' was, of course, only a suspicion. It cannot be denied that Brinkley's behaviour at Maxwell Road on the evening of 19 December was distinctly odd, and the police obviously suspected murder when they requested the Home Office to order an exhumation. But, according to the evidence of Augusta Glanville, the signatures of the 'witnesses' were not on the disputed will when Brinkley showed it to Caroline and herself, which rather suggests that the old lady's death took him by surprise. So all that can really be said on the matter is that he *may* have murdered Mrs Blume – with his usual carelessness – but likewise may not have done so at all.

In other respects, Ingleby Oddie's account is far from accurate. He says, for example, that Brinkley had tricked *both* 'witnesses' into signing the will, and therefore decided that they would both have to be 'disposed of' in order to prevent the fraud being discovered. So he could not have known that Heard had written the will himself, or that he had testified to having been present when Mrs Blume signed it.

Though others who have written accounts of the case – e.g., C. Ainsworth Mitchell – have not made such claims as this, they have all accepted without question that Parker was tricked. Indeed, they seem to have believed that if Brinkley was guilty of the crime for which he was hanged – as he clearly was – then Parker *must* have been telling the truth. The idea that he may have been involved in the fraud, but lost his nerve when he heard that the will was to be disputed, seems not to have occurred to any of them. Yet that is a far more plausible explanation than Parker's own story.

Parker, after all, was less than scrupulous. There had been complaints about his dealing methods, and he was not above contemplating a fraudulent bankruptcy. So it would hardly have been out of character for him to sign the forged will, if Brinkley managed to convince him that there was no danger of the crime being discovered. Nor would it have been out of character for him to try to extricate himself from the case when he heard that the will was to be contested.

Moreover, if we go on to suppose that Parker suspected Brinkley of poisoning the old lady – whether he actually did so or not – then other aspects of the case are not difficult to understand. Parker's undrunk whisky, his unfinished tea, his sudden change of abode and his acute depression can all be attributed to the dilemma in which he suddenly found himself. He was frightened that he, too, would be poisoned, but could not admit this without revealing the reason for it.

The outcome of it all, as far as he was concerned, was not a happy one. His dilemma was over and he had no charges brought against him, but his performance in the witness-box had been unconvincing, and the cross-examination had left him wholly discredited – as was pointed out in the petition for Brinkley's reprieve.

Three weeks later, after Brinkley had been hanged, Parker wrote a letter to the *News of the World* from 269 Brighton Road, Croydon, where he was then living. In this he said that he was in a pitiable state, that he was without work and that the strain of the trial had unnerved him. He appealed to his friends for assistance, but whether they gave him any we do not know.

Probably, by this time, he had very few left.

THE STRANGE AFFAIR OF THE LYONS MAIL

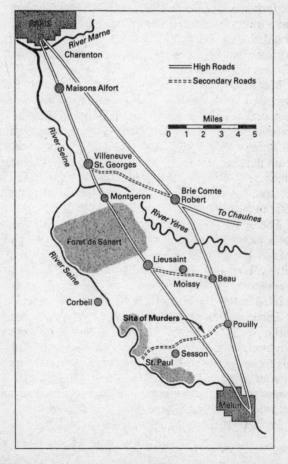

A section of the Paris to Lyons High Road and its surrounding area, showing the site of the Lyons Mail Murders of 1796.

1. Murder on the Melun Road

On the afternoon of 27 April 1796, the Lyons Mail left Paris heavily laden with articles of value, including a large consignment of Government money packed in wooden boxes. It had, as usual, no escort or guard – just a courier with two pistols and a postilion who was not armed at all. The only other person travelling in the coach was a sullen passenger without luggage who had booked his place giving the name Laborde.

The courier, Jean-Joseph Excoffon, had been running a regular service to Lyons – a distance of over 250 miles – for several years. The journey took about thirty hours, with the postilion and the horses being changed every ten or twelve miles, and letters and packages delivered all along the route. The passengers – on the few occasions that there were any – rode with Excoffon at the front of the coach.

The first change of horses took place at Villeneuve St Georges, where on this occasion a postilion named Étienne Audebert took over from Nanteau, the fellow who had driven the vehicle from Paris. Up to this point, Laborde, who wore a grey overcoat with a sabre underneath it, had been sitting with his hat down over his eyes, as if pretending to be asleep. He did not speak to anybody as the changes were made.

A few miles further on, at Lieusaint – south of the Forest of Sénart – the courier handed a packet of letters to the postmaster's son, to whom he mentioned that he had a passenger who was sulky and whose looks he did not like. Neither Excoffon nor Audebert were seen alive

53

again after the mail had left Lieusaint.

The following morning, the bodies of both men, together with the wrecked mail coach and two of the three horses, were found near the village of Pouilly, about three and a half miles from Melun. The vehicle had been waylaid by a party of horsemen (as hoof-prints at the scene showed); the courier and the postilion had been brutally murdered, and almost all of the money had been stolen. It was a horrifying crime.

Excoffon, a married man aged fifty, had died in his seat, having been stabbed three times in the chest and stomach and slashed on the side of the neck with a sword. Audebert had suffered many injuries as he tried to escape on foot: one of the blows had severed his right hand, another had split his skull. The coach had afterwards been moved to the edge of a nearby field, where the courier's body was pushed out onto the ground and the culprits searched the boxes and packages, leaving a mass of debris. Their haul was enormous.

The Government money which they carried off comprised seven million francs in *assignats* (a paper currency worth only a small fraction of its nominal value), 742,000 francs in *mandats territoriaux* (a second paper currency, of greater value than the first), and 10,000 francs in gold and silver – all of which had been on its way to Italy, to finance a military campaign which General Bonaparte was conducting there.

Other articles of value stolen from the coach included several thousand francs in coins, more paper money and a quantity of jewellery and silver plate. These had all been *en route* to different destinations.

There was no sign of the mysterious passenger at the scene of the crime, and it was soon discovered that he had used a false identity card in order to buy his ticket for the coach. Clearly, he had been involved in the crime and had left with his accomplices, riding the missing horse.

The horse was later found straying in the middle of Paris.

2. Couriol and his mistress

When the crime was reported an examination of the scene took place and investigators began questioning people who lived in the surrounding area. The inquiry was conducted by Jean Beau, the senior Justice of the Peace at Melun, who learnt that four horsemen had been behaving suspiciously in the vicinity the previous evening. They had been seen earlier in the day in the village of Montgeron, near Villeneuve St Georges, where they visited first an inn and then a café. Later, in Lieusaint, they again went to an inn, one of them having first taken his horse to the local smith to have a lost shoe replaced.

The Lieusaint innkeeper and his wife informed the police that one of the party, a fair-haired man, had had a broken spur, and had asked for some string to mend it. On being shown a broken spur found beside the courier's body, they both said that that was the one; it had evidently been broken again during the course of the crime.

The same innkeeper told the police that some time after the men had left one of them returned alone, saying that he had left his sabre in the stables. The innkeeper went to the stables with him, and together they found the weapon in a dark corner. But the man then said that he had some time to spare, and told the innkeeper to unbridle his horse and give it some oats while he went back inside the inn to have another drink.

Having asked casually what time the Lyons Mail passed through Lieusaint, the man eventually left in great haste just before it arrived.

*

There was at first no clue to the identity of any of the four horsemen, and the passenger Laborde – against whom a summons had been issued – likewise proved untraceable. But the Paris police, who had been asked by their colleagues in Melun to make certain inquiries, learnt that on the morning after the crime, at about four or five o'clock, a travelling merchant named Étienne Couriol had left four tired horses at a livery stable in the city. These had been taken away by two other men a few hours later.

As a result of this piece of information, Couriol, a native of Avignon aged about twenty-eight to thirty (though he claimed to be only twenty-three), and his mistress Madeleine Breban, who was about twenty, were arrested late at night on 8 May at a house in Château-Thierry, while *en route* from Paris to Champagne. Over a million francs in *assignats* and *mandats territoriaux* was found in a wallet in Couriol's possession, and a search of his van resulted in the discovery of a large strong-box containing a sabre, two pistols, a large sum of money in gold and silver coins, some silver plate and jewellery and various other articles of value.

At the time of these arrests, Charles Guénot, an employee of the Military Transport Board, was questioned, as he, too, had been staying overnight in the same house. He denied knowing anything about the affair, but the arresting officer, an inspector named Heudon, was suspicious of him. He therefore said that he was taking Guénot's papers and luggage to be examined at the Central Police Bureau in Paris.

But as the inspector and his prisoners were about to return to the capital, Guénot suddenly asked for permission to accompany them, as he wished to get his effects back as quickly as possible.

Heudon agreed to let him.

3. Drama at the Central Police Bureau

The prisoners were held in Paris and an examining magistrate for the Pont Neuf section of that city began his own inquiry into the Lyons Mail murders, to the annoyance of those working on the investigation in Melun.

Judge Daubanton lost no time in ordering three more arrests: those of Pierre Thomas Richard, a twenty-eight-year-old general dealer living in Paris, at whose house Couriol and his mistress were known to have stayed from 29 April to 6 May; Couriol's servant or handyman, Antoine Philibert Bruer, who had stayed at the same house not only while they were there but also since their departure, and Marie-Monique Richard, the dealer's wife.

Of these, the first two were held in custody, but the third was released when it became evident that she knew nothing about the crime.

On the day following these fresh arrests, some of the *assignats* found in Couriol's wallet were identified by cashiers of the National Treasury as having been among the money stolen from the mail. Their serial numbers proved that, unlike most of the other *assignats* which had been stolen, they were new notes which had been packed and sealed in one of the wooden boxes straight from the printing press. It therefore seemed almost certain that Couriol was one of the culprits.

The day after that there was a development which was far more dramatic. The police authorities in Melun, at the request of Judge Daubanton, had sent some of their witnesses to Paris, to see if they could recognize Couriol as one of the four horsemen. Among them were Marie Grossetête, a waitress at the *Chasse* inn in Montgeron, and Marie Victoire Sauton, a maid working at the café opposite, both of whom had served the four men on the afternoon of 27 April.

These two women were in the main hall of the Central Police Bureau, waiting for Daubanton to call for them, when they suddenly became agitated and told one of the court ushers that they had to see the magistrate at once, on a matter of life and death.

Moved by their excitement, the usher took them to see Daubanton, who questioned them separately. They both claimed that two men who were at that moment loitering in the hall had been among the party of horsemen they had seen in Montgeron on the afternoon before the crime. They each signed declarations to that effect and, when Couriol was placed before them, identified him as another of the four.

Couriol was sent back to his prison cell protesting his innocence, and the magistrate ordered the two men from the waiting-hall to be brought before him, one at a time.

The first proved to be Charles Guénot, the man who had travelled to Paris at his own request with Heudon and his prisoners.

4. Guénot and Lesurques

Daubanton had at first been disinclined to believe that either of the men in the hall had been involved in the crime, for murderers were not normally found sitting outside his office of their own accord. But Guénot's replies to his questions soon began to give cause for suspicion.

Guénot, aged thirty-three, lived in Douai, but had been staying in Paris for the last two months. He explained this sojourn by saying that he was searching for a carrier named Morin, who had disappeared with three boxes of silver for which he (Guénot) was responsible.

He then admitted that since his arrival in Paris he had been staying at 27 Rue de la Boucherie – the home of Pierre Richard, where Couriol and Madeleine Breban had stayed for eight days after the Lyons Mail murders.

He claimed, however, that he had not known Couriol before 29 April, and that although he was afterwards found in Château-Thierry, in the very house in which Couriol was arrested, they had arrived there on different days, neither of them expecting to see the other. Their presence in the same house at the same time had been merely a coincidence, he said.

As for his presence at the Central Police Bureau that morning, he said that he had come to demand the return of the papers and luggage which had been taken for examination.

To Judge Daubanton the story was unconvincing and, far from getting his effects back, Guénot was placed under arrest.

The examining magistrate then ordered the second man, Joseph Lesurques, to be brought into his office.

*

Lesurques, whom Guénot had described as 'a very old friend and schoolfellow' from Douai, was a married man with three children. He had served for some years as a soldier in the army of the *ancien régime,* and later, while employed as a senior clerk by the Republican municipality of Douai, had made himself a fortune out of buying and selling the confiscated estates of aristocrats who had fled the country. Now, at the age of thirty-three, he had an estate of his own at Douai, and lived in Paris on the income which this provided.

On being questioned by Judge Daubanton, he said that he and Guénot – 'the oldest of friends' – were always in touch with each other when Guénot was in Paris, but that he had not been with him on 27 April and had never been riding with him outside Paris. He admitted that he knew Pierre Richard, who was also from Douai, but not that he had the reputation of being a receiver of stolen property. He also admitted that he had met Couriol – though he did not know him by that name – at Richard's house.

'What was Richard's business?' asked Daubanton.

'When he lived in Douai he was apprenticed to a jeweller,' replied Lesurques. 'Since he came to Paris I have lost sight of him. He may be a jeweller still, but I cannot say.'

Lesurques was then arrested and searched, and two civic identity cards were found in his possession, neither of which had been issued to him. One was that of his cousin André Lesurques, a forty-four-year-old master tailor living at a different address in Paris, which the prisoner said must have been left at his own home by mistake. The other had no holder's name at all – though it bore an official stamp and the names of witnesses – and Lesurques claimed to have found it among a lot of loose papers which he had bought.

He had no card of his own – in spite of being bound by law to carry one – and, on being asked to account for this, said that he had never bothered to get one. He was never out late at night, and so was never likely to have to produce one, he declared.

5. Couriol betrayed

A further arrest took place shortly afterwards, that of David Bernard, a thirty-six-year-old Jewish general dealer suspected of being a large-scale receiver of stolen property. Bernard was known to have had dealings with Couriol, and to have sold him the van in which he and Madeleine Breban travelled to Château-Thierry. There was also evidence that the four horses believed to have been used in the crime had originally come from – and later been returned to – a livery stable which he owned.

Judge Daubanton thus had seven suspects in connection with the affair, and from 12 May to 23 May he was busy questioning and confronting them with witnesses.

The easiest of them to deal with was Madeleine Breban, who soon began to make accusations against Couriol in her determination to save herself.

Madeleine had lived and travelled with Couriol for ten months. She said that prior to 27 April they had been staying at a lodging-house in the Rue du Petit Reposoir, where he received many business associates, but did not allow her to be present while he was seeing them. On the day of the murders he went out without her, saying that he was going into the country, and did not return until the following day. On 29 April the couple moved to Richard's house in the Rue de la Boucherie.

When she was shown a broken and bloodstained sword which had been found at the scene of the crime – having evidently been broken while being used to open the wooden boxes – Madeleine said that Couriol had had one just like it. He had lost it and replaced it with another – the one found in his van at Château-Thierry, she told Daubanton.

Then, on being asked how Couriol had been dressed before and after the murders, she said that as far as she could remember he had been wearing a blue coat, a red embroidered waistcoat, buckskin breeches and a three-cornered hat with a gold band and tassel. As one of the four horsemen had also worn an embroidered waistcoat and a three-cornered hat, this was regarded as an important piece of evidence.

Madeleine had, in fact, been so forthcoming that Judge Daubanton took the unusual step of releasing her on parole – though not without intimating that this was to induce her to make further revelations.

Bruer, Couriol's fifty-three-year-old servant, had little or nothing to reveal. Although two witnesses said that they had seen him in Lieusaint shortly before the murders, this was clearly in error. Bruer, who gave the impression of being simple, had been with Madeleine at the house in the Rue du Petit Reposoir on the night of 27

April, and told the magistrate that he knew nothing about the crime in question.

Bruer had been in domestic service before the Revolution, and had afterwards become destitute. He said he believed that Couriol had employed him out of pity, as he, too, had been born in Avignon.

Couriol himself seemed unperturbed by the amount of evidence which was accumulating against him. He denied having been away from Paris on the night of the crime, and, on being asked how he had come by the silver plate found in his strong-box, replied that he had bought it from a man he did not know, 'somewhere near the Barrière des Sergents'.

He agreed that he had taken four horses to a livery stable on the morning of 28 April, but said that these belonged to four business associates whom he had met on the bank of the Seine. He had not ridden them himself, he declared.

As for the matter of the broken sabre, this, too, failed to ruffle him. 'Oh, yes!' he said, when the weapon was produced. 'That is the one with the inscription on it, of which I spoke. I swapped it away two months ago, to a man whose name I cannot recall. How the blood got on it, or how it was broken, I have not the slightest idea!'

Later, when presented with the official record of his examination, Couriol refused to sign it, claiming that he could not read or write.

*

The next two prisoners to be questioned were David Bernard and Pierre Richard. Both clearly knew more about the affair than they cared to admit, though neither appeared to have been among the main culprits.

Bernard, who denied that any of his horses had been used in the attack, was proved to have spent a lot of money – mainly on commodities such as brandy and wine – during the days that followed it.

Richard, who had put Couriol up – together with his mistress and servant – for the eight days beginning on 29 April (and had also procured a false passport for him), had been further incriminated by the discovery of hidden money and valuables in his home.

The last two, Guénot and Lesurques, both appeared from the evidence of witnesses to have been among the four horsemen seen in Montgeron and Lieusaint before the crime. Neither of them had been found to be in possession of any of the proceeds – though it was said that Lesurques had been spending more money than usual – but the evidence of identification seemed overwhelming.

Lesurques, for whom the wife of the innkeeper at Lieusaint claimed that she had mended the broken spur, declared that he had not left Paris on the day of the crime and that he had not ridden at all since his arrival there almost a year earlier. He accused the various witnesses who had identified him of malice and impudence.

*

On 22 May the conduct of the inquiry was removed, by means of a summons, to Melun, where the legal authorities were determined to deal with it themselves. Daubanton was compelled to send them his prisoners, together with all the evidence which had been collected, and his proceedings were annulled on the grounds that he had omitted certain formalities. They were then started afresh by Judge Beau.

The prisoners continued to deny having been involved in the crime, and all claimed to have alibis. Having heard and interrogated each of them, Beau examined the witnesses from Montgeron and Lieusaint, including several who had not been examined by Daubanton. At the end of June, after reading his report, a grand jury decided that the six men should all stand trial.

However, on choosing counsel, the accused were advised to ask for the trial to be held in Paris, as they were entitled to do, on the grounds that local prejudice was against them in Melun.

They did so, and duly appeared before the Criminal Tribunal Court of the Seine a month later, on 2 August.

6. An arrogant and self-satisfied man

The trial was dominated by the presiding judge, Louis Jerome Gohier, an arrogant and self-satisfied man who made no attempt at impartiality. It lasted four days, with eighty-six people appearing as witnesses.

The indictment contained a detailed account of the crime. It alleged that the courier had been stabbed by the passenger Laborde, whose whereabouts were still unknown, and that each of the prisoners had either taken part in the attack on the mail or had known about it and received a share of the proceeds.

Following the reading of this document, which took an hour, the accused all pleaded not guilty to the charges against them. Lesurques, at this point, declared that his indictment was absurd, as he could prove that he had been in Paris on the night of the murders, and this led to an argument between Gohier and himself about the witnesses who claimed to have seen him in Montgeron or Lieusaint. The trial then proceeded.

The first witness to be called was Madeleine Dolgoff, a middle-aged widow with whom Excoffon and Laborde had had a meal in a restaurant before leaving Paris on the afternoon of 27 April. She remembered the passenger's features and identified a grey overcoat found at the scene of the crime as the one which he had worn.

The two cashiers from the National Treasury and a merchant named Raynouard then identified some of the paper money found in Couriol's possession as notes which had been in the mail at the time of the attack. In each case, it was argued by the defence that the money could have changed hands several times during the eleven days between the crime and Couriol's arrest.

Before long, the witnesses from Montgeron and Lieusaint began to appear. Jean de la Folie, an ostler employed at the *Chasse* inn, identified Couriol and Lesurques as two of the four men whose horses had been left in his charge; he did not recognize any of the other prisoners. A farmer named Perraud, who had dined at the inn while they were there, said that he, too, recognized Couriol and Lesurques (though he was not certain about the latter) – and also that Guénot had been another of the four men.

Of the two women who had been responsible for the arrest of Lesurques and Guénot at the Central Police Bureau, Marie Grossetête, the waitress at the *Chasse*, was prevented by illness from giving evidence. But Marie Victoire Sauton, the maid from the café opposite, again identified them both. She said that the four horsemen had all visited the café and that Lesurques and Guénot had played billiards together. Lesurques had tried to pay the party's bill with a 1000-franc *assignat* note, but she had objected to this and one of the others had paid her in silver instead.

Charles Alfrey, a nurseryman, said that he had seen two men walking arm-in-arm along the street in front of his premises in Lieusaint, and believed that one of them – whom he had at first mistaken for one of his neighbours – was Lesurques. Alfrey's wife was much more certain: she told the court that she had seen the two men walk past the premises together three times that afternoon, and was sure that one of them was Couriol and the other Lesurques.

This led to another altercation. Lesurques claimed once again that he had never been to Lieusaint, and

65

Gohier told him that his denials would not prove his innocence in the face of 'all these recognitions by witnesses from the Melun road'. When Lesurques said that the witnesses were deceiving themselves, Gohier made an accusation of his own.

'The reports about you are far from satisfactory,' said the president. 'The police report that at the time of the outrage you had no regular status in Paris, that when you were arrested you had neither a passport nor a civic card – so that you were a citizen neither of Douai nor of Paris. The authorities in your native place say that you made a fortune sufficient to maintain yourself easily, but that you were a dissolute and a spendthrift.'

And when the shocked victim of this attack protested that he was a family man, Gohier pointed out that Lesurques had a mistress, and said that he had been spending heavily since the crime.

Eventually the hearing of evidence was resumed, and Jean Champeau, the innkeeper at the *Cheval Blanc* in Lieusaint, and his wife both identified Couriol and Lesurques as two of the four horsemen. They said that Couriol was the one who, having left the inn with the others, had returned for his sabre, stayed for a drink, and then left hurriedly just before the arrival of the mail. As for Lesurques, he was the man with the broken spur, which the innkeeper's wife had mended for him.

On being asked whether he could identify any of the other accused, Champeau replied that he did not recognize Richard or Guénot, but that Bernard may have been one of the other horsemen. His wife said the same thing about Bernard, adding, 'I think it was he who dropped a white handkerchief on the steps of the inn and stooped to pick it up.'

At this, Bernard interrupted, saying that the witness was mad. He always used yellow handkerchiefs, had never slept outside Paris, and had not left his house on 26, 27 or 28 April, he declared.

But these remarks served only to irritate the witness, who then said, 'I am not a madwoman. The more I look at you, the more I seem to know you. You were wearing the same Dutch-cut coat with red facings that you are wearing in the court today!'

The last witness of the first day was a cattle dealer named Gillet, who had seen the four horsemen in the street in Lieusaint. He, like Alfrey, had mistaken one of the men for a neighbour, and he, too, thought that Lesurques was the man in question, though he could not be sure of it. He also thought that he recognized Couriol as another of the four.

7. The goldsmith's daybook

The following day, the remaining prosecution witnesses gave their evidence. Humbert, the stableman with whom Couriol had left four horses on the morning of 28 April, was among them. But the most important was Madeleine Breban, who had managed to save herself at her lover's expense.

Madeleine said once again that Couriol had been out on the night of the murders, and identified the broken sword as the one which he had recently owned. She also said that she had often seen Richard, Bernard and Guénot in his company, but claimed that she knew nothing about the crime itself or the sharing of the proceeds.

After Madeleine had given evidence, the first defence witnesses appeared. An attempt was made on Couriol's behalf to show that he was well-known and regarded as well-to-do in certain circles. But he had no satisfactory alibi for the day of the crime, and the result was unimpressive.

The first witness to appear for Lesurques was Legrand, a goldsmith and jeweller with a shop in the Palais Égalité. Legrand said that he had seen Lesurques almost every day for some months, and that on 27 April the prisoner had been in his shop from about 9.30 in the morning till 1.30 in the afternoon. He went on to say that he was sure of the date on which this had happened, because while Lesurques was there he had had a visit from another jeweller named Aldenhoff, who had bought a silver pocket-spoon and sold him a pair of earrings.

As the witness said that these transactions had been recorded, the president asked to see his daybook. The book was produced by Lesurques's counsel, and Gohier began examining it. He found that the transactions had indeed been recorded but that the date of the entry had been altered.

Pointing this out, Gohier accused Lesurques of trying to mislead the court. He then had a short discussion with his four colleagues before ordering Legrand's arrest for forgery.

Thereafter, another fifteen witnesses were called on the same prisoner's behalf, but none of them could have made such an impression on the minds of the jurymen as the discrediting of Legrand's evidence.

The painter Hilaire Ledru stated that he and Lesurques had dined together on the evening of the crime, and afterwards met Guénot in the Boulevard des Italiens. The three men then went to a cafe, and afterwards visited André Lesurques, the prisoner's cousin, at his house in the Rue Montorgueil, said Ledru.

The master tailor and his wife both corroborated this story, but the jeweller Aldenhoff, who appeared next, said that he, the prisoner and Ledru had all dined at André's home that evening.

Several other witnesses said that they thought they had seen Lesurques in the street that day, but proved not to be certain of it.

The last witness for this prisoner was Eugénie Dargence, a girl of twenty who had been his mistress for several months. Eugénie said that Lesurques had called in to see her on the evening of the murders, as he did every day. But Gohier, questioning her at length, threw her into a state of confusion and destroyed the effect of her evidence.

The second day's proceedings thus ended with Lesurques's defence falling apart – and the presiding judge had still not finished with him.

8. Legrand in a state of terror

On the third day of the trial, with the public benches suddenly more crowded than before, witnesses were called to establish alibis for the next three prisoners, David Bernard, Pierre Richard and Philibert Bruer. Bernard, the Jewish general dealer, sought to prove that he had been seen in various parts of Paris on the day of the crime; Pierre Richard, the suspected receiver, claimed to have been 'out on the road', though he was unable to explain why he had helped Couriol after the crime or how he had come by the hoard of money and other valuables found in his house; and Bruer, Couriol's servant, had evidence that he had spent the night at his employer's lodgings with Madeleine Breban.

However, those members of the public who had been drawn to the courtroom in the hope of witnessing further sensations were not in for a disappointment. Before any defence of the last prisoner, Charles Guénot, could be offered, Legrand was brought back into court to face questions about the falsified daybook which had been produced the previous day.

Terrified at the prospect of being in serious trouble, he informed the court that before receiving a summons to appear as a witness, he had had a call from Guinier, Lesurques's counsel. The advocate had looked at his daybook and told him that because of the entry concerning his transactions with Aldenhoff he could bear witness that he had seen Lesurques on the day of the crime.

'And do you now persist in your original declaration?' asked Gohier.

'No, I withdraw my original declaration, which was based on the false date in my daybook,' replied the goldsmith. 'I did not realize that it had been tampered with until yesterday.'

He went on to say that the book was always lying open on his counter, and that he was sure that neither he nor his wife had altered the date in it. 'I cannot imagine how the alteration was made,' he said. 'I swear that it was not I who made it.'

Then, on being asked whether any of the other defence witnesses had based their own depositions on the same falsified entry, Legrand answered, 'I know that Aldenhoff and Hilaire Ledru gave evidence similar to my own because of the date which they saw in my book, and I suppose the same was the case with Baudart, though I am not sure.'

He could not convince the president of his failure to notice the alteration, for it was obvious to anyone who saw it that one figure had been written over another. It was therefore suspected that Legrand had conspired with several other people, including Guinier, in an attempt to help Lesurques. However, he was later acquitted of the forgery and released.

With his defence now demolished, Lesurques was asked whether he had any observations to make about the entry in Legrand's daybook. Close to breaking down, he stammered, 'I can only ask the citizens on the jury to disregard the depositions based on the false date.'

When Legrand had been removed from the court, Guénot was given an opportunity to present his defence. It could not have seemed likely that he would produce a satisfactory alibi, for he had been found staying at the same house as Couriol in Château-Thierry, had stayed

70

for a long time at Richard's house in Paris, and had been identified by witnesses from Montgeron. However, he countered the prosecution's evidence in a surprising manner.

He said that on 27 April, after returning to Paris from Champagne, he had dined with an official of the Central Police Bureau with whom he had been in touch for some time over his search for the three missing boxes of silver. The official, named Clement, duly appeared to confirm this, showing that Guénot could not possibly have taken part in the attack on the Lyons Mail.

Later the same day, following a long adjournment, the prisoners were all asked if they had anything to add to the evidence which had been produced on their behalf; none of them had. The Public Prosecutor then made a long speech, withdrawing nothing and demanding the conviction of all of the prisoners, irrespective of the evidence of Clement. This was followed by a series of speeches for the defence, as the accused all had different advocates, except Bernard and Bruer, who had one to represent them both.

All these speeches kept the court in session until 2.30 in the morning. Because of this, the fourth day's proceedings did not begin until the comparatively late hour of ten o'clock.

9. Three convicted of murder – including Lesurques

In making his own address to the jury, the presiding judge did little more than repeat the arguments of the prosecution and give a warning about the dangers of highway robbery. Even so, when the jury retired to consider their verdict, they did not return for six hours. Finally, at 8 p.m., the results of their deliberations were announced: Couriol, Lesurques and Bernard were all guilty of premeditated murder and robbery, Richard was guilty of receiving part of the proceeds of the crime, and

Guénot and Bruer were not guilty.

Before passing sentence, Gohier asked those who had been convicted whether they had anything to say. There were two speeches.

'Doubtless the crime of which they accuse me is a dreadful one, and deserves the death penalty,' said Lesurques. 'But if murder on the highway is abominable, it is equally abominable to turn the forms of law to strike down an innocent man.'

He went on to say that the day would come when his innocence would be proved, and that the guilt of his blood would then rest on the heads of the jurors and the presiding judge.

In view of Lesurques's other protestations of innocence, this sort of thing was only to be expected. But the other speech, from Couriol, took everyone by surprise.

'Lesurques and Bernard are innocent!' the speaker declared. 'Bernard only lent the horses and got some profit, while Lesurques had nothing to do with the affair.'

Couriol, Lesurques and Bernard were sentenced to death, the judge ordering that they be taken to the place of execution wearing red shirts, as the law prescribed. Richard was sentenced to twenty-four years' penal servitude, and to be exposed in the pillory in a public place for six hours. The judge also ordered the confiscation and sale of goods owned by the prisoners, to compensate the State and private individuals for money and valuables stolen from the mail.

The condemned had, however, the right to appeal to the Court of Cassation, the supreme court of France, and all of them did so without delay.

10. Protests from the tumbril

Couriol's declaration at the end of the trial was followed by two further statements, in which he admitted that he had been involved in the affair and repeated his claim that Lesurques and Bernard were innocent. He named as his accomplices Jean Guillaume Dubosq, a well-known robber and jailbreaker residing in the Rue Croix des Petits Champs; a man named Lafleur who lived in the Rue de Valois; an Italian named Roussy, living in the Rue St. Martin; and Jean Baptiste Laborde, alias Durochat, whose home was in the Rue de Charonne. He also said that Madeleine Breban knew all of these men and that she had known about the plan to rob the mail.

None of the four men thus accused was found in Paris, and Couriol's account of the crime contained many details known to be untrue, undoubtedly intended to confuse his own part in the crime. It was even suspected that he had falsely accused others in his attempt to save Lesurques and Bernard. But the case had by this time received a lot of attention, with newspapers hinting that not everybody was satisfied with the outcome of the trial. A magistrate attached to the Central Courts was therefore given the task of investigating any fresh evidence which might come to light before the condemned men's appeals were heard.

A certain amount of fresh information *did* come to light in the weeks that ensued. A lodging-house keeper informed the magistrate that he had entertained a man named Lafleur, better known as Vidal, prior to the crime, and described two other men with whom this Lafleur had been in contact. And Madeleine Breban, no longer denying that she had known of the planned robbery, agreed that she knew Lafleur, Roussy and Dubosq, and gave descriptions of all three of them. It appeared from her new disclosures that Lesurques, a fair-haired man, had been mistaken for Dubosq, who had auburn hair but sometimes wore a fair-haired wig.

But when the appeals of the condemned were heard on 8 October, they were all rejected, the Court of Cassation stating that they had not provided any grounds for quashing the decision of the lower court.

*

Couriol, Lesurques and Bernard then appealed to the Directory which at that time governed France. The Directors referred the case to the Council of Five Hundred, one of the country's two legislative assemblies, requesting that body to review it, and the Council appointed a commission from among their own members to carry out the task. The prisoners were accordingly granted a further reprieve, to await the result.

The commissioners searched for evidence that a miscarriage of justice had occurred. But after perusing all of the documents relating to the case, they came to the conclusion that the decisions of the two courts of justice had been correct.

Lesurques and Bernard, at their trial, had tried to refute the evidence of respectable witnesses by producing false or worthless ones of their own, the commissioners observed. Having failed to do so, they had tried unsuccessfully to impress the appeal court with extra-judicial evidence which was not at all convincing.

The commissioners duly reported their findings to the Council of Five Hundred, recommending that the condemned should be left to their fate – and the Council concurred.

On 27 October, Lesurques and his counsel drew up a final appeal to the President of the Council. But no attention was paid to it, and the following day his wife and children were allowed to see him for the last time. The harrowing scene which then occurred was recorded in a picture by Hilaire Ledru, whose own evidence at the trial had failed to help him.

On the morning of 30 October 1796, the three condemned were taken in a tumbril to the Place de la

Concorde, the place of execution. Lesurques had obtained permission to wear white clothes, as a protest against his condemnation, and Couriol – who was resolute and had dressed with care – called out several times to the spectators, 'I am guilty, but Lesurques is innocent!' Bernard lay on the floor of the cart, weeping and muttering all the way.

When he arrived on the scaffold, Lesurques protested his innocence for the last time. 'I am not guilty, but I pardon those who judged me,' he said to the officials in attendance.

He managed to remain calm, in spite of being the last of the three to suffer.

11. Durochat's confession

Though the Court of Cassation and the Council of Five Hundred had been certain that Lesurques was guilty, others were convinced that he had been convicted in error. These included Guinier, the dead man's legal adviser, who criticized the Government for allowing a judicial murder to take place, and – far more surprisingly – Judge Daubanton, who blamed himself for what he now regarded as a tragic mistake. It was Daubanton's desire to see justice done – insofar as it could now be done – which led to another new development in this strange case a few months after the three executions had been carried out.

On 12 March 1797, Daubanton learnt from a list of prisoners that a man named Joseph Durochat was in the Ste. Pelagie prison, about to stand trial for theft. Knowing that Durochat was one of the names used by the sullen passenger involved in the Lyons Mail murders, he went to watch the man's trial, taking with him a supervisor of the mails who had been present when Excoffon started out on his fatal journey. The prisoner was found to match witnesses' descriptions of Laborde, and the magistrate's companion confirmed the similarity. So, having seen him convicted and given a sentence of fourteen years' penal servitude, Daubanton arranged to have the man placed in his own charge.

Durochat was confronted with a number of other witnesses who had been present when Excoffon left Paris for the last time. These included the widow Madeleine Dolgoff, with whom the courier and his passenger had had a meal in a restaurant, and Jean Maurice Excoffon, the courier's seventeen-year-old son, who had called at the mail-yard to see his father off. All of them recognized Durochat as the mysterious Laborde, and although he denied it and said that he had not been anywhere near Paris or Melun on the day of the murders, Daubanton was sure that they were not mistaken.

The prisoner was accordingly handed over to the authorities in Melun. But on appearing before the criminal tribunal there, he, too, exercised his right to choose his place of trial, saying that he wanted it to be held in Versailles. Daubanton had therefore to be recalled from Paris – accompanied by his usher and two gendarmes – in order to transport him there.

When they arrived at Versailles, Durochat, alias Laborde (his real name was Joseph Verot), made a long statement, admitting that he had taken part in the attack on the Lyons Mail but disclaiming responsibility for the murders which had been committed. He named Dubosq as the organizer and Couriol, Louis Roussy, alias Beroldi, and Pierre Vidal (an alias of Lafleur, whose real name was Pierre Pialin) as the other three men involved.

Dubosq, according to Durochat's account, had learnt from an official at the Central Postal Bureau that the Lyons Mail leaving Paris on 27 April would be carrying a large sum of government money intended for General Bonaparte's 'Army of Italy'. He told Durochat and Vidal of a plan to rob it and, when they agreed to help him, took them to meet Couriol and Roussy, who had already been recruited for the same purpose.

Durochat went on to say that he had agreed to travel in the coach and overpower the courier, but had not taken part in either of the murders. He claimed that when the ambush took place Couriol had stopped the coach and cut down the postilion and that Vidal had murdered the courier in a green lane behind some trees – to which spot Durochat confessed that he had helped to drag him.

Later, when they got back to Paris, the gang went to Dubosq's rooms in the Rue Croix des Petits Champs, where Bernard joined them and was given a share of the money for providing the four horses.

Lesurques had not been concerned in the crime in any way, and Durochat said that he did not even know anybody of that name.

12. Bribery in a police van?

Though Durochat's account confirmed Couriol's claim that Lesurques was innocent, it also contained certain statements in his own favour which were unlikely to be true. In particular, his description of the murder of the courier could not be believed, for the grey overcoat found at the scene was bloodstained in such a way that the person wearing it – Durochat himself, according to several witnesses – was almost certainly the one who had inflicted the fatal wound.

Moreover, when he appeared before a local examining magistrate, Durochat told a different story, this time stating that Excoffon had been killed by Roussy and that he himself had been injured in the thumb while trying to defend him. He even showed a scar on his thumb in the vain hope of convincing the justice that he was telling the truth.

Durochat was sent for trial and duly appeared the following month. Vidal, in the meantime, had been arrested in Paris for another crime, and on learning of his capture, the Versailles judges demanded that he be sent to them for examination. He was thus confronted with Durochat at the latter's trial, but although Durochat identified him immediately, Vidal denied knowing Durochat. An altercation then took place between the two men who, according to Durochat, had been friends since 1793.

The trial ended on 6 April with the prisoner being convicted and sentenced to death. A large sum of money which had been found in his possession was confiscated, and part of it was used to compensate the courier's widow for the loss of her husband.

While Durochat was awaiting the result of his appeal to the Court of Cassation, Dubosq was arrested near Moulins. Arrangements were made for him to be sent to Melun for trial, as that was where the original warrants of arrest had been issued, and the authorities there asked for Durochat to be sent to them as well, so that he could appear as a witness. He was therefore sent under guard to Paris, where, astonishingly, he and Dubosq were put into the same police van, to be taken to Melun together.

When the two men were confronted with each other in Melun, Durochat said that the man before him was not Dubosq. 'The man against whom I have given evidence had a fuller face than the man I see now,' he declared. 'He was also taller, though both have fair hair.' He added, as if genuinely concerned to see justice done: 'I identified Vidal without difficulty and I could identify this person, too, if he were the right man – but he is not.'

Nothing could be done to induce him to change his mind, so he was taken back to Versailles to wait for the outcome of his appeal. Although the money found on him had been confiscated, he was able to spend freely during the weeks which followed his return; apparently his failure to identify Dubosq had been the result of bribery.

Durochat's appeal was finally rejected by the Court of Cassation on 21 July, and he was guillotined on 9 August. Shortly before his death, he admitted that the prisoner in Melun *was* Dubosq, and that his false statement to the contrary had been planned between them. He also declared that Lesurques and Bernard had both been innocent of the crimes for which they were condemned.

13. A chance to escape

Pierre Vidal, Jean Guillaume Dubosq and Claudine Barrière – Dubosq's mistress, who had been arrested with him – were held in Melun for some months, but had finally to be handed over to the judicial authorities of Seine-et-Oise, of which department Versailles was the prefecture.

Vidal, a dark man with receding hair, a red 'bleary' eye and black whiskers, had been sentenced to twenty years' penal servitude in Grenoble in 1794, for highway robbery with violence, but managed to escape after serving only one year.

It was known that he had been in Paris prior to the Lyons Mail murders, and that Durochat had frequently visited him in his rooms in the Rue de Rohan; it was also known that he had left shortly afterwards, saying that he was going to Lyons, where his father was dying.

The evidence of identification in his case was not very clear, for some of the witnesses from Montgeron and Lieusaint confused him with Guénot, who had been able to produce an alibi for the night of the crime. But there could be little doubt that Vidal was guilty, for Durochat and Couriol had both named him as an accomplice in their confessions, and neither had had anything to gain by accusing him falsely.

Dubosq, a good-looking man with a humorous disposition, was well known in criminal circles. He had several times been sentenced for theft or burglary, but invariably escaped – the first time from the galleys at Toulon, on other occasions from prisons in Paris, Rouen and Lyons. His reputation as a daring and resourceful underworld figure was thus established long before the attack on the Lyons Mail.

Dubosq was similar to Lesurques in appearance, especially when he wore a fair-haired wig. But he was hardly his double, and most of the witnesses who had identified Lesurques as one of the four horsemen refused to accept that they may have been mistaken. However, he had been named by both Durochat and Couriel, and so it seemed that he, like Vidal, was almost certainly guilty.

Claudine Barrière, a skilled pickpocket, had been Dubosq's mistress for several years. She was tall, thin and by no means attractive, but he was devoted to her – so much so that on the occasion of his last escape (from the prison in Lyons, where she was also being held), he had broken into the women's side of the prison in order to take her with him.

Claudine was known to have been in Dubosq's company about the time of the Lyons Mail murders, and there was evidence that she was guilty of certain lesser offences in connection with that affair. So when the authorities in Seine-et-Oise demanded that the other two prisoners be sent to them for trial – on the grounds that Durochat's case, with which they were connected, had already been dealt with in Versailles – they naturally insisted on their right to try her as well.

Dubosq, Vidal and Claudine Barrière were handed over in August 1797, and taken initially to Pontoise. There the proceedings which had been conducted in Melun were repeated, as Judge Beau was regarded as having had no legal authority to conduct them. Later, on being sent for trial, the prisoners were removed to Versailles, where they were still in jail towards the end of

February the following year. By this time they were intent upon staying no longer.

The prison was run in a relaxed, almost casual manner, and Dubosq – who always had money at his disposal – had had no difficulty obtaining the various implements which he needed in order to escape. On 26 February, after locking-up time, he let himself out of his cell and unlocked Vidal's door. He and Vidal then forced open an iron-barred gate and went up to the top corridor, where they released Claudine and used the same skeleton keys to open a door leading to an attic room in the head turnkey's apartments.

The room, which was on the third floor, was used as a bedroom for the children of the household, whose mother was known to have taken them to stay with friends in Pontoise. The three prisoners were therefore able to work uninterrupted, making a rope out of sheets and curtains in order to lower themselves to the pavement below. Before long, Vidal climbed down the rope and made good his escape.

Dubosq went next, leaving his mistress to follow, but while he was on his way down one of the knots came undone. He fell twenty feet or more to the pavement, and lay there helpless, perhaps unconscious, until discovered by the midnight patrol.

Claudine, in the meantime, had abandoned her own attempt to get away and returned to her cell.

*

Dubosq was placed in a cell on the first floor, with both of the bones of one leg broken and his other leg badly lacerated. The prison doctor at first had doubts about whether he would recover, but Claudine was given permission to stay in the cell with him, and this had a beneficial effect on his morale.

After two and a half weeks the danger of gangrene

had passed and the broken bones were showing signs of mending. Dr Du Clos then felt able to report that nature was making a great effort in the prisoner's favour, and Claudine was allowed to be Dubosq's nurse.

However, it was accepted that it would be months before he was well enough to stand trial, and there was no question of Claudine being tried without him. As for Vidal, he could not be found.

14. Dubosq's secret recovery

Having recovered from the shock of his fall and the pain of his operations, Dubosq complained of extreme tiredness, weakness and inability to use his legs. The doctor, at his request, allowed a pulley to be fixed to the ceiling, so that he could use it to sit himself up for his meals. But for a long time he seemed to be in a state of complete exhaustion.

In fact, he was making a faster recovery than Du Clos realized. Within a few months, while still apparently bedridden, he was able to get up and do exercises during the hours of darkness. Then, still without arousing suspicion, he and Claudine once again began making preparations for an escape.

The cell which they occupied had a large fireplace which was not used during the summer months. Dubosq began loosening its fire-back by removing the mortar from around it, and soon it could be moved. He then started cutting the mortar from between the stones of the outer wall, replacing the fire-back each time he finished work, in order to hide what he was doing.

Finally, on the night of 16 August, he made a hole large enough for them to squeeze through, and he and Claudine – using a rope made from bed-curtains and the cords of Dubosq's pulley – climbed down into a private garden below the cell.

They got away safely before dawn, and their disappearance was not discovered until the turnkeys unlocked the cells at six o'clock.

Over two years elapsed before they were recaptured.

*

Vidal remained at large for only three months, and was back in prison long before Dubosq was fit enough to make his own escape. His arrest took place in Lyons, at the home of a professional thief, on 5 June, and he was taken back to Versailles on 19 July.

At his trial, he once again claimed that he knew nothing about the attack on the Lyons Mail and that he had never had anything to do with the two men who had named him in their confessions. However, he was convicted on 8 September, and his appeal was rejected six weeks later.

He was guillotined on 2 December the same year.

15. Dubosq and Claudine recaptured

Following their own remarkable escape, Dubosq and Claudine remained together, and were still living as man and wife when they were recaptured in Paris in September 1800. By this time, Dubosq's jailbreaking exploits were legendary and many regarded him as a romantic hero, in spite of the widely-held belief that an innocent man had been executed in his place. Even so, it was only as a result of an anonymous letter to the Prefect of Police that his presence in Paris became known, so not all of his acquaintances could have thought too highly of him.

At the time of their betrayal, the couple were living in apartments in the Rue Hautefeuille. Dubosq was not at home when a party of police officers arrived there, and Claudine pretended not to know his whereabouts. But a close watch was kept on the neighbourhood and he was apprehended the following day.

He was taken back to Versailles and placed in irons, his jailers allowing him to see nobody except his legal advisers. In December, he and Claudine were brought to trial, surrounded by gendarmes.

The case was still one of great interest to the public, and the court was crowded during the four days that the proceedings lasted. The bill of indictment suggested that Joseph Lesurques had been the victim of a miscarriage of justice because of his resemblance to Dubosq, and much of the first day was taken up with the witnesses who had appeared on his behalf four years previously. These included the goldsmith Legrand, who was said to have suffered a 'nervous crisis' and had to spend part of the intervening period in an asylum; he was still not able to explain the alteration in his daybook. The rest of this group of witnesses could only repeat the evidence which they had given in 1796.

Then, on the second day, the witnesses from Montgeron and Lieusaint appeared. Of the nine whose evidence had sent Lesurques to the guillotine, all but one denied having identified him in error, saying that they did not recognize Dubosq. At one point President François Chollet asked Marie Victoire Sauton, the maid from the café in Montgeron, if she realized that she had identified Charles Guénot in error, and whether she might not have made an equally grave mistake in identifying Lesurques.

'No, I do not think so,' she replied, her self-assurance unshaken.

Peraud, the farmer, who had also mistakenly identified Guénot, declared, 'I do not think that I was in error when I identified Lesurques. On the contrary, I cannot identify the man here today, whom you call Dubosq, as having been one of the party at the inn. Although he is about the same height as Lesurques, and his hair is much the same colour – auburn, shading off into blond – it is not true blond like the other man's. Moreover, his features are quite different from Lesurques's.'

The only one to waver was Marie Alfrey, the wife of the Lieusaint nurseryman, who ended by saying merely that she could not swear that Dubosq had been one of the horsemen.

So the second day's proceedings were almost entirely in Dubosq's favour, and on leaving the dock he spoke to the gendarmes in a jocular manner, asking them whether all the trouble which had been taken to catch him had not been a waste of time.

But the prosecution still had the confessions of Couriol and Durochat as proof of his participation in the murders, and there were various witnesses to give evidence of his association with these offenders, both before and after the crime. The third day's proceedings were therefore not at all favourable to him, and he frequently interrupted them with cynical remarks or outbursts of anger.

The receiver Pierre Richard, who was serving twenty-four years' penal servitude for his own part in the affair, was one of these witnesses. He told the court that Dubosq had been one of the gang responsible for the crime and that the proceeds had been shared out in his rooms in the Rue Croix des Petits Champs. The other members of the gang had afterwards accused him of distributing them unfairly, Richard declared.

Madeleine Breban, who was now married to the public executioner of Dijon, deposed that while she was living with Couriol, Dubosq had been a visitor at their lodgings. On the morning after the murders, Couriol had sent her a message, asking her to bring a clean suit of clothes to him at Dubosq's rooms, she continued.

When she did so, she was met at the door by Claudine, and shown into a room where Couriol and Dubosq were both waiting. She gave Couriol the clean clothes and took away the suit which he had been wearing.

Further witnesses were produced to give evidence of Claudine's association with Dubosq. These included their landlord in the Rue Croix des Petits Champs, who said that the couple had left their rooms a few days after the murders, and that he had afterwards found some ashes in a hole under the flooring, indicating that something had been burnt in haste.

On being asked to explain the presence of burglary tools in their apartments in the Rue Hautefeuille, Dubosq said that he had thought about crossing to England and committing acts of sabotage in revenge for the blowing-up of French ships at Toulon. He then claimed that successive Ministers of Justice and Judge Daubanton had conspired against him.

Later, a fair wig resembling Lesurques's hair was placed on Dubosq's head, and the witnesses from Montgeron and Lieusaint were asked to look at him again and see whether this gave them any cause to reconsider the depositions which they had made the previous day. They all said that it did not, except Marie Alfrey, who now told the court that she had made a mistake in identifying Lesurques in 1796, and that Dubosq was the man she had seen on the day of the crime.

This astonishing change of testimony, from a woman who admitted that she had been too frightened to make it the day before, threw Dubosq into a rage. He accused the witness of lying and said that she had been suborned by 'the friends of Lesurques'. If she wasn't lying, then all the other witnesses *had* lied, he argued. The outburst continued until Chollet suddenly declared the session closed.

On the fourth day, the jury heard the speeches for the prosecution and the defence, followed by a summing-up from the presiding judge which was hostile to the accused. They were then given a list of thirty-seven questions to consider, and told that their verdict must depend upon what answers they gave to these.

The jury retired for only two and a quarter hours before reaching a unanimous verdict. Dubosq, they decided, was not guilty of either of the murders, but was guilty of aiding and assisting the murderers, with premeditation. Claudine Barrière – also referred to as 'la femme Dubosq' – was not guilty of that offence, but guilty of concealing stolen goods, with criminal knowledge.

Dubosq was sentenced to death, his mistress to twenty-four years' penal servitude; Claudine was additionally sentenced to stand in the pillory in a public place for six hours. An appeal to the Court of Cassation was dismissed and Dubosq was guillotined on 23 February 1801. He had spent the two months since his condemnation in chains, and died without making a confession.

The verdict was a blow to the hopes of those who believed in Lesurques's innocence, for it was not inconsistent with the outcome of the first trial. If Dubosq had organized the attack on the mail but not been present when it took place, Lesurques could still have been one of the murderers. So, having hoped for a verdict which would vindicate the dead property-owner, Lesurques's widow, Judge Daubanton and many others had good reason to be disappointed. However, they remained convinced that their cause was a just one and refused to despair. During the years that followed they were as active as ever in their struggle to clear Lesurques's name.

16. Roussy in a Spanish prison

Louis Roussy, alias Luigi Beroldi, the last of the men named by Couriol and Durochat as their accomplices in the crime of the Lyons Mail, remained at large for another two years. A tall man with a large red birthmark

87

on his right hand and wrist, he had already been known to the police in Paris at the time of the murders, and left to return to his native Italy shortly afterwards. Later, in 1803, he was found to be in prison in Madrid, having been concerned in robberies in a number of churches.

A request was made for his extradition, and he was handed over to the French police in Bayonne. From there he was taken to Versailles, where he denied being the wanted man but was identified by a former mistress and various other people, including several of the witnesses from Montgeron and Lieusaint. He was brought to trial in February 1804, convicted of murder, and guillotined on 30 June.

On the day before his execution, he entrusted to his confessor a short written statement in which he admitted his guilt and declared that Lesurques had been innocent. At his own request, it was not revealed until January the following year, but its publication then caused a renewal of agitation from those who believed that Lesurques's conviction had been a mistake. A large body of public opinion was still unconvinced that justice had been done.

However, when the Emperor Napoleon, in 1806, received a number of petitions from members of the Lesurques family and their supporters, requesting an examination of the whole affair, his Minister of Justice could see no grounds for agreeing to this, and the matter was dismissed.

Jeanne Lesurques lived until 1842, making one attempt after another to clear her husband's name. She was eventually compensated for the losses which she and her children had suffered through the confiscation of their property, but only after many years of hardship. She never succeeded in establishing that her husband had been convicted in error.

Lesurques's daughter, Mélanie D'Anjou, and her son Charles also made many attempts to obtain a revision of the judgment, but these, too, were unsuccessful. None of the governments to which they appealed was ever convinced that Lesurques had been innocent of the Lyons Mail murders, and so it was never officially acknowledged that a miscarriage of justice had taken place.

A French melodrama, *Courrier de Lyon*, which made its first appearance in 1850, was loosely based on this affair. But its ending, from Lesurques's point of view, was far happier than it had been in real life.

It was very popular.

17. The witness who admitted her mistake

The affair of the Lyons Mail thus resulted in five criminal trials, seven executions and seventy years of controversy kept alive by regular bursts of agitation. Various authors have written accounts of it, some arguing strongly that Lesurques was innocent, others accepting that he may not have been. The evidence is by no means conclusive either way.

Of the seven men who were executed, six had been found to have taken part in the murders. This was one too many, as only the four horsemen and the passenger had been present when the crime was committed. But the bill of indictment against Dubosq had conceded that David Bernard, though he had certainly 'participated with the murderers in the division of their spoil', had *not* been involved in the crime itself.

So it was accepted that the jury at the first trial had returned an erroneous verdict in one case, even if that was not the case of Lesurques. Had they not done so, Bernard might reasonably have expected a sentence similar to Richard's – i.e., a term of penal servitude – rather than the death penalty. But this point was overshadowed by the more serious question of whether Lesurques had been executed for a crime with which he had had no connection whatsoever.

Of the other five convicted of murder, three had admitted taking part in the crime, each stating that Lesurques had been innocent. Others associated with the gang, such as Pierre Richard and Madeleine Breban, had made similar declarations. Although these were all infamous characters whose motives were regarded as suspect – no credence was given to their statements for this reason – they had nothing to gain and may well have been speaking the truth.

Lesurques was clearly not the respectable, law-abiding family man he tried to make himself out to be: his association with Eugénie Dargence, his possession of two civic identity cards which had not been issued to him, and his false alibi, based on a falsified document, were all proof to the contrary. Nor were his unexplained daily visits to the goldsmith Legrand's shop necessarily innocent.

He was, in fact, rather an unscrupulous person, and there is good reason to believe that at the time of the Lyons Mail murders he was engaged in some sort of underhand business which he was not willing to reveal.

Yet, leaving aside the evidence of the local people from Montgeron and Lieusaint, there are no grounds for believing that Lesurques was closely associated with any of the other people charged in connection with the crime except his friend Charles Guénot, whom he had accompanied to the Central Police Bureau when he went to demand the return of his belongings.

None of the stolen property was found in his possession, and there was no evidence of it having passed through his hands. There had, admittedly, been rumours of his spending a lot of money during the ten days prior to his arrest. But Lesurques had a considerable income from his estate in Douai: twelve to fifteen thousand francs in silver (equal to millions in depreciated *assignats*), according to his own statements on the subject. So if he had been spending heavily during the days leading up to his arrest, this was not proof that he had had more than usual at his disposal.

It cannot be denied that Lesurques was identified as one of the horsemen by a large group of country people, and that when these witnesses were later confronted with Dubosq all but one of them insisted that Lesurques was the man they had seen on the day of the murders.

From this it might appear that Lesurques was indeed guilty of the crime for which he was condemned. But several of these witnesses are known to have been seriously mistaken in other respects.

David Bernard's conviction for murder rather than a less serious offence was due to evidence given by the wife of the innkeeper Champeau. This witness mistakenly accused Bernard of being one of the horsemen, adding that the coat he was wearing in court was the same one as he had worn on the day of the crime. It was this woman's evidence alone which sent Bernard to the guillotine instead of penal servitude.

The two women who denounced Lesurques to Judge Daubanton, and the farmer who had seen the horsemen at the *Chasse* inn, all confused Charles Guénot with Pierre Vidal. Had Guénot not had a strong alibi for the evening of the crime, he, too, would almost certainly have been convicted as a result of their depositions.

So the evidence of some of these witnesses is by no means reliable, and one is inclined to wonder if, knowing that they had already been mistaken in one case, they could really be sure that they had not been mistaken in another?

Lesurques, though not Dubosq's double, certainly bore a resemblance to him – probably as close a resemblance as that of Guénot to Vidal. Yet Marie Alfrey, the one witness to change her testimony after seeing Dubosq wearing a fair wig, confessed that she had at first not dared to speak out.

Bearing this in mind, we may be justified in suspecting

that some of the other witnesses could have made similar confessions, but refused to do so because they were frightened of being held responsible for Lesurques's death. Or, more likely, that they *had* identified him in error, but were unable to admit such a terrible mistake even to themselves.

COLDBLOODED MURDER IN A
DESOLATE PLACE

The Snowy Rowles Case

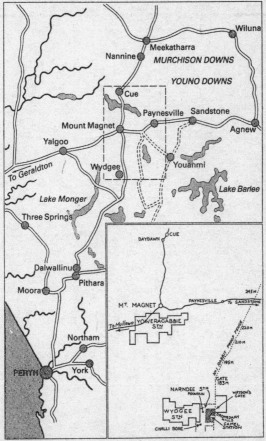

Part of Western Australia with (inset) a sketch map published at the
time of Snowy Rowles's trial. The first human remains were found to
the west of the rabbit-proof fence, near the 183-mile gate.

1. The missing bushmen

In August 1928, a fair-haired young man arrived on a motorcycle at Dromedary Hill Camel Station, in the Murchison district of Western Australia, looking for work. Stanley or 'Snowy' Rowles, as he called himself, was a fugitive from justice: a convicted burglar who had escaped from jail in Dalwallinu while waiting to be sentenced. But he could ride a horse as well as anyone else in that part of the state, as he proved by giving a demonstration, and so was offered a job as a stockman on the neighbouring Narndee Station, where he remained for over a year.

Besides being good at his work, Rowles was helpful, good-humoured and sociable. He got on well with the pastoralists, station hands and gold-diggers of this sparsely-populated area, and one man who knew him at this time – the mystery writer Arthur Upfield – later recalled that his appearance at a bush camp 'at once vanquished depression' among the other people present. None of his new acquaintances seems to have suspected that he had anything to hide, and it was not until 1931 that his past was revealed. By then he had become the central figure in a dramatic murder case.

*

The 'Murchison Mystery' began in December 1929, when James Ryan, a middle-aged well-sinker, and George Lloyd, an accordion-playing South Australian of thirty-two whom he had just taken on as his mate, disappeared from Ryan's camp on Narndee Station after being seen in Rowles's company.

Ryan had been working at Narndee since January, and was fencing off a supply of water at a part of the station called Challi Bore when the mate he had then, a half-caste boy named Bell, left him in November. Ryan then left his work unfinished and drove off in his utility truck to Burracoppin, a small wheat town to the south where he met Lloyd.

Snowy Rowles had also left Narndee in November, intending to make his living by trapping foxes and dingoes in the same locality. But on 4 December, or thereabouts, he visited Dromedary Hill, to make inquiries about Ryan, claiming that Ryan and he had agreed to go on a trip to the north-west together. A day or two later he set off towards Burracoppin – 163 miles away – in search of him, driving an old car which he now owned.

The car broke down and had to be abandoned a hundred miles north of Burracoppin, but Rowles continued on foot and found Ryan, Lloyd and a man named George Ritchie at a camp four miles further south. He drove back with them to Dromedary Hill, and they all stayed the night of 7 December at the camel station homestead.

In the morning, Rowles left for Challi Bore, twenty miles to the south-west, with Ryan and Lloyd, and the following day he and one other man – apparently Lloyd, though Rowles later denied this – went to fetch the abandoned car. They left it in a shed at Dromedary Hill, then went off again to Ryan's camp.

On 10 December, Charles Herman Bogle, the part-owner and manager of Narndee Station, went to inspect the work at Challi Bore and found Snowy Rowles at the camp on his own. Rowles told him that he was now working for Ryan, and that he had come back to camp to prepare a meal. Bogle stayed to have lunch with him, but saw no sign of either Ryan or Lloyd.

Three days later, Rowles rode up to the Narndee Station homestead on his motorcycle and asked Bogle for a motor-repair outfit, which he said he wanted for Ryan. But on 21 December, when he next went to Challi Bore, Bogle found the place deserted and the camp gone.

That Ryan and Lloyd had both disappeared soon became obvious. But as they belonged to Australia's large floating population, nobody saw any need to report them missing; it was merely assumed that they had gone somewhere else in search of work.

So over a year elapsed before anyone began to suspect that they had been murdered – and in the meantime a third man disappeared.

2. Pieces of bone among the ashes

Leslie George Brown, a twenty-seven-year-old man known in the Murchison as Louis J. Carron, had arrived in Australia in February 1930. He had previously lived in New Zealand, having migrated from Canada some years earlier, and was married in Auckland in December 1925. He changed his name to Carron when he left New Zealand, by which time he and his wife had separated.

He reached Fremantle by boat about 6 February, having had all of his money stolen on the voyage, and while in Perth during the next day or two met a man named John Lemon, who had travelled on the same boat from South Australia. After discussing the problem of finding work, Carron and Lemon made their way to the Murchison together.

When they got there, they went from one sheep station to another, and before long Carron found work at Wydgee, adjoining Narndee Station on the west, and Lemon was taken on at Narndee, to fill the job that Rowles had left vacant. The two men were close friends by this time, and so kept in contact with each other during the months that followed.

Rowles was still in the surrounding area, and had Ryan's truck with him. After leaving Challi Bore, he had worked for two or three months at a hotel in Youanmi, a small town to the east of Dromedary Hill, but had since gone back to trapping. He explained his possession of the truck in various ways, sometimes claiming that Ryan had sold it to him.

Getting to know Lemon, he became a frequent visitor to his old outcamp, and while there on 13 May heard that Carron, who had been given notice, was about to leave Wydgee and intended coming over to see Lemon himself. Rowles told Lemon that he would like to have Carron as his mate, as trapping was a lonely job, and two days later turned up at Wydgee to fetch him in the truck he now called his own.

Carron was paid off with a cheque for £25 0s 7d, but he and Rowles remained on Wydgee Station until the next day, when they both left in the truck. They arrived at Lemon's outcamp between seven and eight o'clock in the evening, with the skins of some kangaroos which they had shot on the way, and stayed with him for a day and a half.

On the morning of 18 May, Rowles and Carron got ready to leave, saying that they were going to look for work in the goldmining town of Wiluna, about 200 miles to the north-east. Before they left, Carron's camera was used to take photographs of all three men.

Carron was by this time in the habit of writing to Lemon regularly when they were apart, and promised to send him fruit from the first town they reached, as well as copies of the photographs which had been taken. But Lemon did not receive either the fruit or the photographs; nor did he receive any further letters from his friend. So he soon became worried and began to make inquiries about what had happened.

On learning, in July, that Rowles was again in

Youanmi, he sent him a reply-paid telegram, asking where Carron was, but got no answer. He later wrote to him, and this time received a reply dated 9 August, in which Rowles claimed that he and Carron had parted company in Mount Magnet – a town about seventy miles north of Lemon's outcamp on Narndee Station – and that Carron had gone to Geraldton. The letter also stated that Rowles had sent Lemon an earlier letter in reply to his telegram.

These claims only served to make Lemon even more anxious than he had been before. But he hesitated to report his friend's disappearance, hoping that Carron would sooner or later get in touch with him. So several more months elapsed before the police began to investigate the mystery, and even then it was not Lemon who initially brought it to their attention.

*

The person who did was a man named Jackson, a friend of Carron's living in Dunedin, New Zealand. Jackson, like John Lemon, had not heard from Carron for some months, and so, in December 1930, wrote to a police officer in Mount Magnet, asking for inquiries to be made about him. On receipt of the letter, Constable William Hearn made a search for the missing man in Wiluna, but could find no trace of him there.

The following month, Lemon finally reported Carron's disappearance himself. Hearn then began making further inquiries, and on 19 February 1931, accompanied by a fellow constable named McArthur, visited an old unoccupied hut on a rabbit reserve about twenty miles north of Dromedary Hill.

The hut stood among dense mulga scrub about 660 yards to the west of the No 1 Rabbit-Proof Fence, a 1130-mile-long vermin fence stretching from Banningarra, on the north-west coast, to Hopetoun in the south.

It had no supply of fresh water, and a bore three hundred yards further to the west was disused and unequipped.

Neither the hut nor the bore could be seen from the road which ran along the fence, but near the bore the two police officers discovered the ashes of a large camp fire, containing, among other things, a human molar and some broken-up pieces of burnt bone which looked like parts of a human skull.

There was a smaller pile of ashes about forty feet from the main one, and when these were examined more pieces of broken-up bone were found, together with a gold-faceted wedding ring, some artificial teeth, a gold clip from a dental plate, a used 0.32-calibre bullet, a cartridge case and other items of interest. All of these articles except the bullet and cartridge case had been burnt, but the grass at this point was not burnt. It therefore seemed that the ashes had been brought over from the main pile when they were already cold.

A third pile of ashes was discovered about 200 feet from the main one, also on unburnt grass, and among them more human and artificial teeth, another gold dental clip, some bone buttons and a number of boot or shoe eyelets were found. The human teeth were badly burnt, but the artificial ones were not damaged at all. Besides all of these discoveries, Hearn and McArthur found a broken camp-oven and a saucepan near one of the piles of ashes, and a soldered petrol tin near the bore. The oven contained traces of ash and burnt bone.

The two constables reported all this to the police headquarters in Perth and, as it was suspected that a murder had taken place, Detective Sergeant Harry Manning was sent to conduct an investigation.

Manning immediately began making inquiries and soon learnt that Carron's cheque for £25 0s 7d had been cashed by Snowy Rowles at a hotel in Paynesville, a mining town to the north of the rabbit reserve, two or three days after the two men left Narndee in Rowles's truck. He also learnt of the disappearance of Ryan and Lloyd five months earlier.

On 1 March, Manning and Hearn went to the rabbit reserve together, and this time a French coffee tin and another lot of buttons, shoe eyelets and artificial teeth were found. The two police officers also noticed a track which showed that a motor vehicle had been driven between the main fire and the bore and back again.

3. Snowy Rowles arrested

Four days later, Manning, Hearn and another constable named Thomas Penn went to Hill View Station, about 140 miles north of Narndee on the Murchison Downs, where Rowles was now working. They found nobody at his outcamp and the hut locked, and so waited until the following afternoon, when he drove up in a sulky. Manning then recognized him as John Thomas Smith, the convicted burglar who had escaped from Dalwallinu three years previously. Rowles did not deny that this was so.

Questioned about the disappearance of Louis Carron, he told Manning that as far as he knew the missing man had gone to Geraldton. Manning then said that he was also looking for the other two men who had disappeared, and asked Rowles to account for a Dodge utility truck which was standing in a shed behind his camp. Rowles said that he had bought the vehicle from James Ryan.

Manning informed Rowles that he was under arrest, but allowed him to cook himself a meal while a search of the hut was carried out. When two 0.32-calibre rifles were found and unloaded, he asked him whether all the articles in the camp were his own property. Rowles replied that they were, apart from the two rifles, which belonged to the owners of the station, a shotgun, an old sewing-machine and a gramophone.

In a drawer of the sewing-machine the police officers

found a pair of hair-clippers, which Rowles said that he had bought from an Afghan hawker named Sher Ali; in another drawer there was a shaving-kit, which he also said was his.

On a high shelf over the head of his bed there was a parcel wrapped in newspaper. When it was lifted down, Rowles said to Manning, 'Where in the hell did you get that? I know nothing about it!' The parcel contained three shirts, a wristwatch, a white-handled razor, a watch-chain and a pair of scissors. Rowles denied all knowledge of them.

Searching the utility truck, the police found an Omega-brand open-faced watch set in the dashboard; this, according to Rowles, had been there when he bought the vehicle from Ryan. They also found an electric torch, which Rowles said he had bought himself.

After he had finished his meal, Rowles was allowed to change his clothes. He was then taken by car to Meekatharra, a distance of eighty miles, and lodged in the local jail. The next morning he was interviewed by Manning and made two statements.

*

The first of these concerned his movements in company with Carron prior to the latter's disappearance. In this he said that when he and Carron left Lemon's outcamp on 18 May, it was with the intention of going to Wiluna. They drove ten miles eastwards to the 164½-mile peg in the rabbit-proof fence – about a mile and a half north of the camel station homestead – then northwards along the fence to the 206-mile gate, where the road between Mount Magnet and Youanmi passed through it.

There, having stopped for a meal, they spent two hours shooting kangaroos before driving to an old unoccupied homestead situated a few miles away on Windimurra Station, the prisoner continued. They then camped in the homestead, going out to lay a trail of poisoned bait for foxes before they settled down for the night.

The following day, instead of going on with their journey, the two men decided to stay on at the homestead for a while and Rowles went to buy stores in Paynesville, about fifteen miles away, leaving Carron to peg out some skins. But when he arrived at the Paynesville Hotel, where the purchases were to be made, Rowles found that Ted Moses, the licensee, was working at a mine that he owned, four miles from Paynesville. Rowles was therefore unable to get the stores that day, and so stayed the night at the hotel.

In the morning, he finally got the stores that they needed, and asked Moses to change the cheque for £25 0s 7d, which Carron – having agreed to pay half the cost of the goods – had entrusted to him. Moses did so by giving Rowles one of his own cheques for £16 and the rest of the change in cash. Rowles maintained that he gave Carron this new cheque and £4 8s in cash when he saw him back at the homestead.

The following night, the two men went into Mount Magnet, where Carron, who was a teetotaller, objected to Rowles drinking and decided to part company with him. Rowles claimed that he then gave Carron £16 in cash for the new cheque, as it had been made out in his own name and Carron was afraid that nobody else would cash it for him.

He concluded his account by saying that a fortnight after seeing Carron for the last time he had received a letter from him, written from Geraldton and accompanied by a copy of one of the photographs taken at Lemon's outcamp. He did not know what he had done with the letter – which, in any case, had not given Carron's new address – but believed that he had given the photograph to Alice Jones, the daughter of the hotel proprietor in Youanmi, he said.

103

In his second statement, dealing with the disappearance of James Ryan and George Lloyd, Rowles said that towards the end of 1929, he travelled southwards along the No 1 Rabbit-Proof Fence by car to meet a man named George Ritchie, and unexpectedly found Ryan and Lloyd with him at his camp, ninety-six miles north of Burracoppin. He stayed overnight with them and Ryan offered him a job at £3 10s a week, which he accepted. But the four men all got drunk, and in the morning neither Ryan nor Ritchie were capable of driving their own vehicles, so he and Lloyd had to do it for them.

Rowles went on to say that Ryan and Lloyd suffered from the effects of drink for three days after their arrival at Challi Bore, so no work was done during that time, and he (Rowles) was able to go and fetch the car which he had abandoned.

'Soon afterwards Ryan and Lloyd went to Narndee homestead and back on the same day, and we started cutting a skyline for a fence,' the prisoner declared. 'Ryan had trouble with his tubes, and I rode my motorcycle, which I had brought to the Murchison with me, to the homestead for repair outfits. On the way back I got to the Fountain camp (his old outcamp), where George Bridges was, and camped the night.

'Next day I returned to Ryan's camp to find a note left by Ryan, saying that they were working two miles south at a bore and asking us to mend the tubes. While I was mending the tubes, Mr Bogle came and dined with me. He offered me a job on Narndee, and asked me where Ryan was. I told him, but he did not got down to them.

'I fixed the truck and returned to Ryan and Lloyd, who were still cutting the skyline. I told Ryan that Bogle had been out and Ryan asked me if Bogle had mentioned an order from Burracoppin. He then explained that he had made a fool of himself at

Burracoppin and left an order at the hotel on Bogle. He did not know how much money he had spent. He said he also got two tyres from Nelson Perce and had not paid for them. Ryan said he would have to do a lot of fencing to get square with Bogle, and we all suggested that we should leave Bogle and go north prospecting.'

Rowles sold his car to finance the proposed trip, and because of this it was understood between them that he now owned a half-share in Ryan's utility truck. The three men then acquired petrol and stores, packed their belongings into the truck, and set out towards the rabbit-proof fence.

They reached the fence at the 164½-mile peg, turned northwards, and went on beyond the Mount Magnet to Youanmi road. But the truck broke down at the 212-mile post, and as they could not get it started again they had to camp there. The following day, while they were still unable to get the truck started, an argument broke out, and Rowles decided that he could stand his companions no longer.

'I took my gear off the truck and placed it in the scrub off the road and walked back to the Youanmi road, at the 206-mile peg,' he told Manning. 'Two northbound cars came along with two men in one and three in the other. Some hours later, at sundown, one car returned with Ryan in it. The men were middle-aged and had been drinking. The car stopped and Ryan called me aside and asked me what I would give him for his share in the truck. I eventually gave him £32 in notes, which with the £18 Ryan owed me (from a recent loan) was £50 for the truck.

'I travelled north with Ryan and the others to where they had left Lloyd in the other car. Ryan and Lloyd then left me, taking their gear on in the two cars towards Wiluna. I did not know the names of the men, but Ryan appeared to.'

Manning later claimed that after signing the two statements, Rowles said to him, 'A man must have a kink to do this sort of thing. I am sorry I did not take my old lady's advice. She wanted me to give myself up when I escaped from Dalwallinu, and if I had taken her advice I would have had that all over by now and would not have this other thing to face.'

On being asked what 'other thing' he was referring to, he allegedly replied, 'Oh, I suppose the less said about that the better!'

*

Following the interview with Rowles, Manning and Hearn went to Narndee Station and carried out a search of Challi Bore. They found no trace of the skyline which Rowles claimed that he and his companions had been cutting, and the station manager was certain that no work had been done at the site while Rowles and Lloyd were there.

During a second search of the area, some months later, the remains of eight fires were found. An examination of these resulted in the discovery of a lot of very small pieces of bone, pieces of an accordion, buttons from vests, coats and trousers, eyelets from boots or shoes, and other items.

4. Two alleged suicide attempts

Though Snowy Rowles was at first charged only in connection with his escape from custody in Dalwallinu, it was afterwards alleged that during the three days which followed his arrest he made two attempts at suicide. The allegation was made as a result of an incident on 9 March, at which Constable Penn and Constable Richard

Fawcett, the keeper of the Meekatharra lock-up, were both present.

According to their own accounts of the incident, the two police officers had just taken the prisoner his tea when they heard a crash coming from his cell and rushed in to see what had happened. They found Rowles lying on the floor with part of an improvised rope round his neck, the other part being attached to a bar across the cell ventilator.

The rope, which had been made from the binding of Rowles's prison blanket, was broken near his neck. It appeared that he had placed a folded mattress on a cell-pan, stood on it and jumped off. 'It's all right now,' he told the two constables. 'I've had two tries and slipped both times. I'll see it through now.'

Evidently hysterical, he went on to tell them that he had tried to kill himself the night before by swallowing strychnine, which he had had hidden in the band of his trousers, but had taken too much and only made himself ill. 'I will never do a lifer,' he said. 'Rather than do time, I hope the —— will string me up. But I will try and hang myself before they get the chance.'

Penn also claimed that two days after this incident, while he was being taken to Perth by train, Rowles said to him, 'What a bloody fool a man is! What a nice mess I'm in! At any rate, I'm not worrying about the Dalwallinu job. Murder is a different thing. The Dalwallinu business is only a flea-bite to what is coming. Anyhow, I'll never do a stretch, as they are sure to fit me on this, and I will swing. I will not get a reprieve, and if the —— do not hang me I will find a way to do it myself!'

*

Rowles was given a three-year sentence for breaking and entering, and so remained in jail while Manning continued his investigation of the 'Murchison Mystery'. This

107

lasted until early the following year and involved much correspondence with the New Zealand police over the identification of objects found at the rabbit reserve, as well as thousands of miles of travelling by car and the writing of many reports and statements. Carron's wife, Minnie Alice Brown, his dentist, Arthur William Sims, and an Auckland jeweller named Andrew Thomas Long all emerged as important witnesses. Another to emerge was Arthur William Upfield, whose own part was to give the affair a 'stranger than fiction' quality.

5. An author's search for an original plot

At the time of meeting Rowles, Upfield, then aged forty, was working as a boundary rider on the No 1 Rabbit-Proof Fence. This had been erected – as had many other such fences in Australia – to keep rabbits and other vermin away from the wheat-belts, and Upfield and other riders were employed by the State Government to keep it in good repair. He thus patrolled his own 163-mile section, stretching from Dromedary Hill to Burracoppin, in a large covered dray pulled by two camels, often seeing no other human being for several days at a time.

Between trips he stayed with George Ritchie, who was then in charge of the camel station, at the Dromedary Hill homestead, a stone building with four rooms and a kitchen, where other bush workers, including Snowy Rowles, were occasionally to be found.

Already an author, though by no means an established one, Upfield did most of his writing at night, sitting in the back of the dray by the light of a hurricane lamp. By May 1929, when he left his fence section for a few weeks to assist in the training of two young camels, he was close to finishing his third novel, *The Beach of Atonement*, and trying to devise a plot for the one to follow. He wanted this to be a mystery story featuring his half-aboriginal detective, Napoleon Bonaparte.

The plot which he finally decided upon required the body of a murder victim to be destroyed in such a way that no identifiable part of it was left. But Upfield had no idea how this could be done in the circumstances which he had in mind. So one night, while playing poker at the homestead, he asked Ritchie's opinion.

Ritchie then told him how *he* would do it. He said that he would take his victim out into the bush, and there shoot him and burn his body on a wood fire. A couple of days later he would return to the scene and sieve the ashes, taking out every metal object and piece of bone which remained. The metal objects would then be dissolved in acid and the pieces of bone crushed to dust in a prospector's dolly-pot.

To this, Ritchie added that he would also burn kangaroo carcasses over the ashes, to conceal the real purpose of the fire.

The idea seemed plausible enough, for the dolly-pot was a familiar object in the Murchison: there was one in the blacksmith's shop at Dromedary Hill. But if the body was to be destroyed so completely, the culprit would have to make a mistake of some sort, or the crime would not be discovered. Upfield therefore offered to give Ritchie a pound if he could think of one fatal error which the character in his proposed novel could make.

Ritchie could not do so, though he gave the matter a lot of thought, and other friends and acquaintances – Snowy Rowles among them – were consulted to no avail. By the time Upfield returned to his fence section, the problem was still unsolved.

He remained on the fence for only a few weeks longer and was then put in charge of the camel station, Ritchie taking over his own job as boundary rider. By that time Upfield had found the solution himself: he had decided that the culprit in his novel would slip up as a result of not knowing his victim's war record. However, he continued to discuss the plot with his fellow bushmen, and one such conversation took place on the night of 6 October 1929, two months before the disappearance of Ryan and Lloyd.

It appeared from the other evidence collected by Manning that Rowles, who was himself present at that discussion, had subsequently turned to murder in real life, and had tried to conceal his crimes in the same way as Upfield's fictitious murderer.

6. Upfield at the inquest

On 7 January, 1932, at Fremantle Prison, Snowy Rowles was charged with the murder of Louis J. Carron. Eleven days later he was taken to the Perth Courthouse to attend the inquest into Carron's death, and there sat between his counsel, Fred Curran, and a police constable throughout the day's proceedings.

The inquest was held by Mr E.Y. Butler, the Warden of the Murchison district, assisted by the Crown Prosecutor, Clifford Gibson, who examined the witnesses, and Detective Sergeant Manning, who had now been in charge of the police inquiry for eleven months. Six witnesses appeared during the course of the day.

The first was the Chief Draughtsman in the Lands Department, who produced a map of part of the Murchison, showing the stations, camps and other sites to which the evidence of other witnesses would refer. The map was accompanied by an enlarged diagram of the site where Hearn and McArthur had found pieces of burnt bone and other objects in February the previous year.

The next witness was Miss Doris Ohde, a former employee of a firm of jewellers in Perth, who identified the open-faced watch and the wristwatch found in Rowles's possession as articles which Carron had sent to her firm, Levinson and Sons, for repair in April 1930. She said that the watches were sent back to Carron later the same month in cardboard boxes of a type which Levinson and Sons normally used for articles to be posted.

Miss Ohde was followed by Herbert Stone, the manufacturer of the boxes, who said that each box had ten flat-wire stitches inserted in it during the course of production. He identified ten burnt and rusty stitches found at the rabbit reserve as having been produced by his firm, pointing out that there was a kink in each of them, caused by a defect in his machine.

Sher Ali, the Afghan hawker from whom Rowles claimed to have bought a pair of hair-clippers, gave evidence after kissing the Koran. He said that he had met Rowles on Narndee Station in April 1930, but could not remember selling him anything.

Dr William McGillivray, the Government Pathologist, said that he had examined several packets of bones handed to him by Manning. One of the packets produced contained fragments of a human skull, but the witness had to admit, in answer to a question from Mr Curran, that he did not know whether they were from the skull of a European or an aboriginal.

Bones contained in a small tobacco tin might have been those of human fingers or toes, though Dr McGillivray said that he could not be certain of it. Objects in a matchbox were burnt human teeth, and others produced were artificial teeth. Pieces of broken and burnt bone in another parcel were too small to be identified.

Arthur Upfield, who no longer worked for the State Government, was the last witness of the day. He said that he had become acquainted with Rowles while working for the Rabbit Department as a boundary rider, and went on to explain how he had found the plot for his mystery novel, *The Sands of Windee*, which had by now been published. Rowles had been present at several discussions on the subject, including the one which took place at the camel station homestead on 6 October 1929, the witness revealed.

Upfield also gave an account of the events leading up to the disappearance of Ryan and Lloyd. He had then been in charge of the camel station, and said that he saw Ryan for the last time when Ryan left the homestead to go to Challi Bore with Rowles and Lloyd on the morning of 8 December, and Lloyd for the last time the following day, when he and Rowles went to fetch Rowles's abandoned car and left it in a shed at Dromedary Hill.

After that, Upfield saw Rowles only once more before seeing him in court. That was on Christmas Eve in 1929, when Rowles was at the Youanmi Hotel and had Ryan's truck with him. Rowles had said on that occasion that Ryan and Lloyd were celebrating Christmas in Mount Magnet and that Ryan had lent him the vehicle.

At the conclusion of the day's proceedings, the inquest was adjourned, the Coroner announcing that it would be reopened in Cue, to the north of Mount Magnet, on 8 February.

By the time it did so, the three witnesses from New Zealand had arrived to give evidence.

7. Haircuts at the camel station

Upfield's evidence was reported at length, and when the inquest was resumed the courthouse in Cue was crowded with station hands, station managers, prospectors and residents of the township. Rowles was again present, as he was to be throughout the inquiry, and again he had his counsel sitting on one side of him and a constable on the other.

The first of this day's witnesses was John Lemon, who told how he and Carron, having arrived in Western Australia on the same boat about 6 February 1930, travelled to the Murchison together and found employment on adjacent stations.

He said that while staying at his outcamp between 16 and 18 May, Carron showed him his cheque for £25 0s 7d in Rowles's presence. The next morning, before they left, Carron and Rowles had photographs taken of themselves standing near the truck.

Although Carron promised to write to him, and to send him copies of the photographs and fruit from the first town they reached, Lemon never heard from his friend again – and his attempts to find out what had happened to him were to no avail.

The witness identified a number of objects, including the two shirts, the wristwatch, the hair-clippers and a 0.22-calibre rifle found at Rowles's outcamp, as being similar to articles which had been in Carron's possession, and a hat more positively as the one which Carron had been wearing on the morning he left Narndee Station. Lemon also said that the gold ring found at the rabbit reserve was similar to a ring which Carron had worn on one of his little fingers.

In reply to a question from Mr Gibson, he said that early in April 1930, Rowles had stayed with him for about seven or ten days on another station called Yoweragabbie, about nineteen miles south of Mount Magnet. During that time, as they both needed haircuts, they went to the camel station and cut each other's hair with the clippers kept for camels about to be branded.

Questioned by Mr Curran, Lemon said that the prisoner camped with him for periods totalling about five weeks. He therefore saw most of Rowles's belongings, but remembered him saying that he had other gear in Youanmi. Rowles went to and from Youanmi between the times that he was staying with him, the witness explained.

Constable Hearn, the only other witness to give evidence that day, said that on 31 December 1930, he received a letter from Mr W.A. Jackson, of Dunedin, New Zealand. It was addressed to the Mount Magnet police and requested that inquiries be made concerning the whereabouts of Louis J. Carron, who had last written to him while working in the Mount Magnet area in May 1930. It described Carron as twenty-seven years old and of medium build, with an erect carriage, a sandy complexion and an abrupt manner of speaking.

The inquiries which resulted from this letter, and from a further report about Carron's disappearance from John Lemon, led to a search of the roads and tracks along part of the No 1 Rabbit-Proof Fence, and an examination of the remains of all fires which Hearn and his companion, Constable McArthur, found in the vicinity. It was during the course of this search that the objects from the rabbit reserve were discovered.

Having given a detailed description of these discoveries, Hearn told of his second visit to the site, in company with Detective Sergeant Manning, and of the arrest of Rowles at Hill View Station a few days later. Finally, he gave an account of the search for James Ryan and George Lloyd, which he said was still going on, in spite of the remains found at Challi Bore.

8. The witnesses from New Zealand

On the third day of the inquest, two other police officers were called. Constable Fawcett gave evidence concerning Rowles's alleged suicide attempts, and Constable McArthur corroborated Hearn's account of the finding of various objects, including human remains, at the rabbit reserve. McArthur was followed by the first of the three witnesses from New Zealand.

Arthur William Sims, a Hamilton dentist, identified Carron from photographs as a former patient whom he had known as Leslie George Brown. Consulting a record card, he told Mr Gibson, 'On 1 August 1929, I made a

114

complete lower denture for Brown, and also filled several upper teeth. On 20 August 1929, I placed a small amalgam filling in the biting surface of one of his upper molars.'

Replying to further questions, the witness said that he remembered Brown's mouth perfectly. 'He was wearing a partial upper denture which consisted of four incisor pin teeth held by two gold bands,' he explained. He identified two of the articles from the rabbit reserve as gold bands used in dental work, and said that the molar which had been found there had a drill hole in exactly the same place as the one which he had filled for Brown.

Andrew Thomas Long, the jeweller, was called next. He said that he remembered seeing Carron's estranged wife, Minnie Alice Brown, in his shop in Queens Street, Auckland, but had destroyed the business records relating to that address since moving from it in March 1927. On being shown the gold ring found at the rabbit reserve, he could only say that it appeared to be one of the faceted wedding rings sold by his firm and that a mark on it showed that it had been cut after leaving the manufacturers.

Mrs Brown, the third New Zealand witness, identified Carron from photographs as her husband, Leslie George Brown. She said that she and Brown had been married in Auckland on 30 December 1925, and lived in that city for about a year. They then moved to Hamilton, where they had 'some domestic troubles' leading to their separation early in 1929 – by which time they had two children, Fay and Desmond.

'When I married my husband, he had four artificial front teeth in his upper jaw,' Mrs Brown continued. 'They were kept in place by two gold bands. He was always speaking of having his lower teeth attended to, but up to the time we separated he had not done so.'

As for the ring, she said that on the Christmas Eve before they were married her husband bought her a faceted wedding ring at A.T. Long and Co's shop in Queens Street, Auckland, but had to have it cut down to fit her finger. He took it back when they separated and wore it on one of his little fingers, she told Mr Gibson. The one produced was very much like the ring in question, had the same markings and fitted her finger exactly.

Mrs Brown also identified the watch found in Rowles's truck as her husband's, saying that she could recognize it by its broken dial.

Questioned by Mr Curran, she admitted that her husband had left New Zealand as a single man, but denied that he had told her he was going back to Canada.

'He was born in Canada?' asked Mr Curran.

'I don't know,' replied the witness. 'I can't remember.'

'Did he never mention Quebec to you?'

'I don't remember.'

'How long had your husband been in New Zealand before you married him?'

'A long time.'

'He was born there?'

'No.'

'Did he not tell you what he was?'

'He told me he was a Canadian.'

'Did he send you any money after he left New Zealand?'

'No.'

'Did he not have the children put in a home?'

'He had them boarded out.'

'Did you ever hear of him through the children or through his relations in New Zealand?'

'I never heard of him after he left New Zealand. I never made inquiries through his relatives.'

The next two witnesses were John Worth, the former bookkeeper at Wydgee station, and Ian Thom, who was now the station manager, both of whom were examined

116

briefly concerning articles which had been in Rowles's possession or among the ashes found at the rabbit reserve. Thom was followed by a boundary rider named Lancelot Bowen Maddison, who had much more evidence to give.

9. Carcasses were not always burnt

Maddison had begun working on the No 1 Rabbit-Proof Fence three and a half years previously, patrolling a section which ran northwards from Dromedary Hill and was thus adjacent to Upfield's section. He said he saw Rowles frequently during the time that Rowles was working at Narndee Station, and was also present when the plot of Upfield's projected mystery novel was discussed at the camel station homestead.

Replying to a question from Mr Gibson, Maddison said that on Christmas Eve the same year, he saw Rowles in Youanmi with a utility truck which he knew had belonged to James Ryan. Rowles told him that he had given Ryan £75 for the vehicle, and claimed to have left him in Mount Magnet with George Lloyd.

Maddison saw Rowles at Youanmi several times after that, though Rowles often left the town to go fox-trapping. He still had the truck, which he had painted blue, and on one occasion said that he still owed Ryan £10 on it. On 6 June 1930 the witness found him camped near the place where he had allegedly murdered Louis Carron less than three weeks earlier. He had the truck with him then, and it was loaded with stores.

Maddison joined him for the night, and later noticed that he had a 0.32-bore rifle: a different weapon from either of the ones which he normally carried. As the rifle had no foresight, he helped Rowles to fix one onto it. Maddison identified one of the rifles from Rowles's outcamp as being similar to the one in question.

The witness continued to see Rowles after that

meeting, and on 31 December 1930 went with Mrs Maddison and two other people – a pastoralist named Mrs Brown and Mrs Brown's son – to visit him at his camp on Hill View Station. When it was time for them to leave, Mrs Brown borrowed Rowles's truck to drive back to her own station at Youno Downs, where the witness stayed overnight. In the morning Maddison found a camera with two undeveloped films inside the truck.

Maddison developed the films himself but left the camera at Youno Downs. Some time afterwards Mrs Brown's son handed it back to him, and he passed it on to Constable Fawcett. It was an English camera with markings which were similar to those on the one produced.

On another occasion Rowles said that the hat he was wearing did not suit him and offered it to Maddison in exchange for a cap. Maddison bought a cap in order to make the exchange, and later gave the hat to Detective Sergeant Manning. It was the hat which John Lemon said Carron had been wearing when he and Rowles left Narndee Station together on 18 May 1930.

Replying to questions from Mr Curran, Maddison agreed that Rowles was a hard and capable worker who could get work easily. He also said that he was himself responsible for keeping the hut on the rabbit reserve in repair, and that he used to visit it about twice a year for that purpose. He only once saw any sign that anyone else had been to the place.

'Did you not once go there with Rowles to destroy some kangaroos?' asked Mr Curran.

'Yes,' said Maddison. 'We went and found sixteen dead kangaroos lying in and around the hut, but we did not burn them then as they were too prime. I eventually came back and burnt them. I dragged them into one heap about three chains south of the hut and burnt them in one fire.'

'Is it usual to find dead kangaroos around that hut?'

THE CROYDON SENSATION.—MRS. BLUME'S BODY EXHUMED.

The exhumation of Mrs Blume's body, as depicted in an *Illustrated Police News* drawing.

An artist's impression of Richard Brinkley, the man with the poisoned stout.

LATEST NEWS.

THE CROYDON MYSTERY.

REMARKABLE STATEMENTS IN COURT.

THE Croydon poisoning mystery was carried on a further stage at the police-court on Monday, when the carpenter, Richard Brinkley, again appeared before the borough Bench on the charge of murdering Mr. and Mrs. Beck and attempting to murder their daughter Daisy and the lodger, Reginald Parker, by drugging some bottled stout with prussic acid.

Mr. R. D. Muir appeared to prosecute on behalf of the Public Prosecutor, and in the absence of Mr. Walter Frampton Brinkley was defended by Mr. Bray.

In his opening statement Mr. Muir said that when all the evidence had been called, he would ask the magistrates to commit Brinkley on the capital charge of murdering the Becks and attempting to murder Daisy, their daughter, and Reginald Parker. The evidence would show clearly, he added, that Brinkley had laid poison in order that Parker should drink it. The Court would have to be satisfied that Brinkley had a motive; and that motive would be made quite clear when the tale of Brinkley's association with Mrs. Blume (whose body was exhumed on Saturday) was told.

Mrs. Blume died with extreme suddenness in December last. She had been an intimate acquaintance of the prisoner for seven or eight years. Latterly she lived in the house at Fulham—No. 4, Maxwell Road —alone with a granddaughter named Augusta Glanville, an actress.

Augusta was in a position to know who her grandmother's visitors were, and she says that although at one time the prisoner Brinkley was a frequent visitor to her grandmother, he had for some considerable time before November, 1906, ceased to be a frequent visitor there. In November, or thereabouts, Brinkley's visits became much more frequent, and he used to go and see the old lady several times a week.

One of many newspaper reports showing how the case unfolded before Croydon magistrates.

John Thomas Smith, alias 'Snowy' Rowles, the central figure of the Murchison Mystery.

MURCHISON MYSTERY

INQUEST OPENED.

NOVELIST'S STARTLING EVIDENCE

RELICS FROM CAMP FIRE.

Dramatic evidence was given by a novelist, the author of a recently published mystery "thriller," when the inquest into the death of Leslie J. Brown, also known as Louis J. Carron, was commenced in the Perth Courthouse yesterday morning.

Carron, one of three men reported missing in the Murchison district early last year, was a Canadian. He is alleged to have been wilfully murdered by John Thomas Smith, alias "Snowy" Rowles, near the 183-mile gate on the No. 1 Rabbit-proof Fence about May 18, 1930. Rowles was present at the inquiry, in custody.

The novelist, Arthur Upfield, told how he obtained the plot for his murder mystery, "Sands Of Windee," from suggestions made by another station-hand, in the presence of Rowles. The plot was woven around the shooting of a man and the disposal of his body by burning it in a camp fire.

Fragments of bone discovered by the police in a camp fire in the Murchison were identified by the Government Pathologist (Dr. W. S. McGillivray) as pieces of a human skull.

The inquest was adjourned to Cue, where it will be re-opened on February 8.

How this real-life murder case made Arthur Upfield famous.

Joe Beard, one of Will Buckley's murderers, and a newspaper report of the attempted execution of Will Purvis.

PURVIS DID NOT DIE.

He Was Hung, But Fell Through The Trap Unhurt.

Will be Arraigned and Sentenced by the Court Again.

Senator McLaurin Received an Ovation at His Old Home.

The New Senator Is Met at the Depot by a Body of Citizens Who Pay Him Distinguished Honors.

MERIDIAN, Miss., Feb. 8.—Information reaches here from Columbia, one of the county sites of Marion, that Will Purvis, who was sentenced to be hung yesterday for the killing of Wm Buckley, was taken to the scaffold at the appointed hour all ready for the final drop. He made a short speech to the crowd declaring that the sheriff was hanging an innocent man. The black cap was pulled over his face, he was put over the trap, the rope placed around his neck, the trigger sprung and he fell through the trap door, the noose slipped over his head before he struck the ground. The sheriff and his attendants took charge of the prisoner and again attempted to put him under the gallows, when the the crowd, largely composed of Purvis' friends, insisted that as he had been hung once, the sheriff had no right to hang him the second time. The sheriff then concluded to stay proceedings and await instructions from the district attorney.

MAN ON DEATH BED CONFESSES MURDER FOR WHICH ANOTHER WAS SENTENCED TO DEATH

Sensational Occurrence of Twenty-five Years Ago Recalled When in in Attempt to Carry Out Sentence of Court Will Purvis Escaped Death by Noose Slipping From About His Neck

Columbia, Miss., Mar. 10.—It was revealed by the Sheriff's office here today that Joseph Beard, who died of pneumonia last Sunday, aged 60, on his farm near this city, confessed on his death bed that 25 years ago he and two other men murdered William Buckley, in this section, for which crime Will Purvis, who now resides in Lamar county, Miss., escaped death by hanging only because the noose about his neck slipped after the trap had been sprung. According to the story, Buckley and a brother, revealed to the authorities information concerning a secret band of "white cappers" who operated in this section more than a quarter of a century ago and William Buckley shortly afterwards was what to death from ambush. This was in 1892.

Purvis was convicted of the murder after a sensational trial and was sentenced to be hanged. The execution was to be public and hundreds were present to witness it. But after the trap was sprung, the noose slipped and Purvis fell from the scaffold unharmed. Many of the spectators, superstitious over the thwarted execution, induced the authorities to place Purvis in jail and an appeal to the Governor resulted in commutation of his death sentence to life imprisonment. Several years afterwards Purvis was pardoned.

Beard, attaches of the sheriff's office said, first confessed his part in Buckley's murder to members of a religious sect which he recently joined in order to clear his conscience. Later when Beard was convinced he was dying of pneumonia, the authorities were notified. Beard, it was stated, gave the names of two other men who he said participated with him in the murder and the authorities said they knew where to locate them, but declined to say whether any action against them was contemplated after the long lapse of years. A brother of the murdered man, N. P. Buckley, lives near Columbia.

Joe Beard's confession, proving that Purvis had been convicted in error.

Willie Francis, who survived the electric chair–but later had to face it again.

Francis Must Die In Electric Chair

Willie Francis, negro, confessed murderer of Mr. Andrew Thomas, prominent St. Martinville druggist, on the night of November 8, 1944, and who escaped electrocution on May 3, 1946, when some mechanical defect happene to the chair, may face electrocution a second time. United Supreme Court last Monday by a split vote of five to four decided that Louisiana may try again to execute the 18-year-old Negro.

Immediately after the first attempt to execute Francis, Governor Davis granted him a reprieve. Francis' attorney then ask the Supreme Court to save him from a second trip to the chair. They said a second attempt at execution would mean double punishment—that it would deny the youth the equal protection guaranteed by the constitution

Monday the Supreme Court gave its decision. Of nine justices, five held that the clause in the constitution forbidding cruel and unusal treatment did not apply in Francis' case—that it did not bar a second attempt at execution where the first attempt failed because of mechanical difficulties.

In St. Martinville, where Mr. Thomas was well known and where Francis is also known, the verdict of the Supreme Court is looked on as just and favorable and the great majority of the population expect to see Francis pay with his life for his cold blooded, premiditated murder.

John Lee of Babbacombe - 'the man they could not hang' - on the morning of his release.

John Lee a few months later.

'No, although I did see kangaroos dead in the bush some distance from the hut on other occasions. I just left them there.'

'Isn't it usual for bushmen to burn dead sheep, cattle and kangaroos found lying about?'

'No, only if they are near a hut.'

The witness admitted that animal carcasses may often have been burnt near huts in the bush, and was afterwards asked whether it would not be foolish to burn evidence of a crime in such a place when there were hundreds of square miles of scrub around it. 'I can't say,' he replied.

Finally, on being shown a pocket-knife which Lemon had identified as being similar to one owned by Carron, he said that it was like one which he (the witness) had once given to Rowles.

With Maddison's evidence concluded thus, the inquest was adjourned until the following day.

10. Events at Challi Bore

The next witness was Charles Herman Bogle, the Narndee station manager, who gave evidence concerning the events at Challi Bore towards the close of 1929. Having employed James Ryan for eleven months from January that year, and Snowy Rowles for fourteen months from August 1928, he was able to provide information about the financial circumstances of both men. To Mr Curran, this was a matter of some interest.

'How much did Rowles earn altogether during the fourteen months he worked for you?' he asked the witness.

'About a hundred and fifty pounds,' replied Bogle.

'He collected various amounts at various times without saying what he wanted it for, did he not?'

'As long as he was in credit.'

'Did you owe Ryan any money when he disappeared?'

'I don't know. He never finished the work.'

'Did he owe you money?'

'Well, according to the entries in my books, he was in my debt for twenty-four pounds, as his work was not completed.'

'Do you think he would have been in credit if he had finished the job?'

'I know he would have been.'

Mr Curran then asked whether Ryan had owed money to Bell, the half-caste boy who had been his mate.

'I have heard so, but I don't know,' said Bogle.

'Some unpaid accounts of Ryan's were presented to you for payment, weren't they?'

'Yes.'

'When Ryan disappeared some articles belonging to you also disappeared, didn't they?'

'Yes, a Prismatic compass and a few other things.'

'Were they ever recovered?'

'The compass was not. The loss was reported to the police.'

Only one more witness was called that day: Mervyn Sydney Brandenburg, a Geraldton chemist. Brandenburg said that he several times did business with Louis J. Carron, of Wydgee Station, through the post, and that on 7 April 1930 he sent him a pair of hair-clippers, two films, some photographs which had been developed and printed and a cable-release for a camera.

The witness also said that the prints matched the camera which Maddison had found in Rowles's truck, and that the hair-clippers were identical to those found at Hill View Station. On being questioned by Mr Curran, however, he agreed that neither the camera nor the clippers were of an unusual make.

11. The suspicious prospector

The fifth day's proceedings began with John Joseph

Wheelock, a former stockman, giving evidence about the arrival of Snowy Rowles at the Wydgee outcamp on 15 May 1930, and the departure of both men together in Rowles's truck the following morning. Wheelock identified a 0.32-bore Winchester rifle found at Rowles's outcamp as being similar to one that Carron took from Wydgee on that occasion.

Wheelock was followed by Thomas Symmons Jay, a pastoralist married to the Youanmi postmistress, who told of the delivery of John Lemon's reply-paid telegram to Rowles in July 1930. Jay, in turn, was followed by Alice Evelyn Jones, the Youanmi hotel proprietor's daughter, who identified a photograph of Rowles standing beside his truck as the only one that Rowles had ever given her.

The next witness was Edward Samuel Moses, the licensee of the Paynesville Hotel, where the prisoner spent the night of 20 May 1930 – or 19 May, according to his own account. Moses said that Rowles bought petrol and other goods from his store to the value of £5 11s 3d, and gave him Carron's cheque for £25 0s 7d, endorsed 'L. Carron', to pay for them. When Moses asked who Carron was, Rowles said that he was 'the fellow who came along with (him)', and that he was waiting back at the place where they had set fox-traps. For his change, Moses gave him about £3 in cash and a cheque made payable to 'S. Rowles or bearer' for £17 – not £16, as Rowles had said in his statement to Manning.

On being asked if Rowles had requested some 0.32-calibre cartridges and he been unable to supply them, Moses said that he couldn't remember. He was then asked whether Rowles had bought some beer from him, and to this he replied, 'He told me he thought he had better take some beer out to his mate, and I gave him a couple of bottles of Globe beer.' Asked whether Rowles's appearance had been any different from usual on the occasion of that visit, he said, 'No, not in the slightest!'

When Moses left the witness box, Jay was recalled. This time he gave evidence that after leaving Paynesville that morning Rowles had turned up in Youanmi: a visit not mentioned in Rowles's statement. He said that Rowles arrived at the post office there between 12 and 12.30 p.m., with two bottles of Globe beer, which he and the witness drank between them. He afterwards drove Jay out to a neighbour's place, where he left two more bottles of Globe. Then, when they returned to Youanmi during the evening, he had another bottle, which he drank on his own.

The witness also said that he had never seen Globe beer sold in Youanmi.

James Henry Jones, the licensee of the Youanmi Hotel, was then called. He said that Rowles was a frequent visitor to his hotel, and often bought goods and cashed cheques there. He stayed at the hotel for thirteen days before leaving Narndee in November 1929, and worked for the witness for two months after the disappearance of Ryan and Lloyd a few weeks later. He then stayed for another thirteen days after arriving from Paynesville on 21 May 1930, and on this occasion paid with Moses's cheque for £17, which he said he had received in payment for some scalps or pelts.

Arthur Aubrey, the next witness, said that in December 1929, Rowles was hard up and borrowed £10 from him. He later exchanged his car – the one that had been left at the camel station – for thirteen fox skins, worth £2 each, and gave six of these to the witness in settlement of the debt.

Aubrey was an employee on Narndee Station. He remembered James Ryan returning from Burracoppin, and Rowles saying that he was going to work for him at Challi Bore. In May 1930, he saw Rowles with Ryan's truck and asked where Ryan was. Rowles said that Ryan had sold the truck to him and gone to Wiluna.

Asked about Ryan's camp, the witness said that it was a tent covered with a fly. In answer to further questions, he said that Ryan appeared to be 'charmed and delighted' with his truck, and that he was not the sort of man to leave his employer without giving notice.

After Aubrey, a prospector named James Yates gave evidence. He said that early in December 1929 he had tea with Rowles at Watson's Gate, at the 164$\frac{1}{2}$-mile peg on the rabbit-proof fence, and saw Ryan's truck standing nearby, loaded with petrol, camp gear and food. Rowles told the witness that he had left Ryan gathering timber to make a yard round a bore three miles to the west and was going back to help him. But when the two men parted company, Rowles set out northwards along the east side of the fence, and this made Yates suspicious enough to examine the tracks of the vehicle the following morning. He then found that Rowles had reached Watson's Gate not from the west, as he claimed, but from the south.

On another occasion, at the end of March or beginning of April 1930, Yates found Rowles fox-trapping near the 183-mile gate on the same fence. He again had Ryan's truck with him, and this time said that Ryan had gone to Mount Magnet or Wiluna.

Another prospector, Edward May, said that he knew Rowles from the time when he worked on Narndee Station. On Boxing Day in 1929 he saw him in Youanmi, where he was working at Jones's hotel, and Rowles then told him that Ryan had sold him his truck for £80 and gone to Mount Magnet. May also said that he had seen Rowles in various places since then, and remembered seeing an open-faced watch and a wristwatch in his possession.

12. He could not pass a hotel

On the penultimate day of the inquest, with a hot wind

blowing clouds of fine dust into the stuffy courtroom, Detective Sergeant Manning gave evidence about the investigation which he had conducted into Carron's disappearance, the arrest of Snowy Rowles and the discovery of objects believed to be the remains of James Ryan and George Lloyd.

Giving his account almost without interruption from Mr Gibson, he read aloud the two statements which he had taken from the prisoner and produced the bones and relics from Challi Bore as exhibits. After being in the witness-box for nearly four hours, he was followed by William Henry Wright, an assayer working on Narndee Station.

Wright said that he knew Ryan and told of his trip to Burracoppin when he suddenly found himself without a mate. Asked whether he had been drinking when he arrived back at the station with Lloyd, the witness replied, 'He was almost in the horrors.'

'Did Lloyd have any musical instrument with him when he came up with Ryan?' asked Mr Gibson.

'He had a new accordion,' said Wright.

'You saw Ryan and Lloyd one night at Challi Bore, I believe?'

'Yes,' replied Wright. 'Just before I left them Rowles came to the bore and told me he intended working for Ryan.' He added that when he left, there was nobody at the bore besides Ryan, Lloyd and Rowles.

Wright identified several exhibits, including the broken camp-oven found at the rabbit reserve, as being similar to articles which Ryan had owned. On being asked about the extent of Ryan's drinking, he replied that the missing well-sinker 'could not pass a hotel'.

Constable Thomas Penn appeared next, corroborating the earlier accounts of Rowles's arrest and alleged suicide attempts, and going on to give evidence concerning his alleged self-incriminating remarks on the train to Perth. There was then a stir in the courtroom as the prisoner himself was called, his name being given as

John Thomas Smith. At this point, Mr Curran rose to address the coroner.

'I had intended to allow my client to enter the box, but owing to the attitude adopted by Detective Sergeant Manning, I have decided that it is impossible to expect Rowles to give evidence,' he said.

'The Coroner and the press have been supplied with a list of witnesses, but when I asked for a list, Detective Sergeant Manning refused it.

'It would be grossly unfair to ask Rowles to answer questions when his counsel is denied the opportunity of learning who is going to be brought along to give evidence.

'I have no complaint against the Crown Prosecutor, who was willing to supply the list until Detective Sergeant Manning objected. My complaint is that Detective Sergeant Manning is wholly to blame.'

'That's not fair,' said Mr Gibson. 'I agreed with Detective Sergeant Manning when he said that it was not wise to give the list.'

Mr Curran then asked the Coroner to extend to Rowles the usual protection in the circumstances and not call him to give evidence.

'He will have to be given an opportunity to give evidence if he wants to,' said Mr Gibson. 'He can be called and given the usual warning. He need not give evidence if he does not want to.'

The Coroner agreed with Mr Gibson, and the prisoner entered the witness-box. After repeating the oath in a hesitant manner, he followed the advice of his counsel in declining to give evidence. The inquest was then adjourned until the following day.

13. Wilful murder, but cause of death unknown

On the last day of the inquest, Rowles had police officers sitting on both sides of him, as Mr Curran had left for

Perth at the end of the previous day's proceedings. There were also constables guarding all the courthouse doorways, as there had been on all the other days taken up by this inquiry.

There were still two witnesses who had not yet given evidence, and before either of them was heard an earlier witness, Constable Richard Fawcett, was recalled. Fawcett this time told of a number of articles which Rowles had left at Hill View Station, but which had not been discovered at the time of his arrest. They included a blue serge overcoat which John Lemon, who was recalled immediately afterwards, put on and identified as Carron's.

The first of the two remaining witnesses was Reginald Walter Whisson, a nephew of George Lloyd. Whisson, a farmer, had been living near Burracoppin in September 1929, when Lloyd was brought over from South Australia by the witness's father and brother. He described Lloyd as 'an expert mechanic', and said that that was one of the reasons why they had brought him over.

'I believe he stayed at your father's farm outside Burracoppin?' asked Mr Gibson.

'Yes,' replied Whisson. 'He went into Burracoppin about 20 November 1929, and there became acquainted with a man named Ryan. About eight or ten days later I saw Ryan and Lloyd preparing to leave Burracoppin for somewhere up north in a motor-truck. They were loading stores. Ryan was then drunk, but Lloyd was sober.'

The witness also said that as Lloyd was on the point of leaving he promised that the family would hear from him about Easter. However, they did not do so, and none of them ever heard from him again.

Peter Morrissey, the last witness of all, was a part-owner of Anketell Station, about seventy-six miles to the east of Mount Magnet. He said that about April or May

1930 he and another man found Snowy Rowles having his tea beside a fire in the bush a short distance from the 200-mile peg in the rabbit-proof fence. He was burning something which he said was rubbish.

Morrissey later took Detective Sergeant Manning to the site and was present when he sieved the ashes of the fire and recovered some objects from them. He also saw Manning take possession of two enamel plates, a frying-pan without a handle, a large saucepan and a dented enamel washing-bowl which had been found under a nearby bush.

The articles in question had already been identified by another witness as being similar to utensils owned by Ryan.

At the conclusion of Morrissey's evidence, the Coroner delivered his verdict. He said that the discovery of part of a human skull and a human tooth and bones in the ashes at the rabbit reserve was proof that a body had been burnt there, and that the dental evidence and the identification of the gold ring found with them satisfied him that the body was Carron's.

He also said that although there was no evidence to show the actual cause of death, which may have been the result of a gunshot wound, poisoning or some other cause, he was satisfied that Rowles was the person responsible for it.

'I find that Leslie George Brown, also known as Louis J. Carron, came by his death at the rabbit reserve near the 183-mile gate on the No 1 Rabbit-Proof Fence on or about 18 May 1930, and I find that Leslie George Brown, otherwise known as Louis J. Carron, was wilfully murdered by John Thomas Smith, otherwise known as Stanley or Snowy Rowles,' he declared.

Snowy Rowles, aged twenty-six, was then committed for trial at the March Sessions of the Perth Criminal Court, and taken away to his cell by three constables. He duly appeared before Mr Justice Draper on 10 March

1932, denying the offence with which he was charged.

14. The rustling overcoat

The trial lasted for eight days and, like the inquest, received much publicity. Almost all of the witnesses who had given evidence at Cue were called again, though the procedure in this court was more formal than that of the inquest and some of the evidence given previously had to be excluded. In addition to these witnesses, there were several new ones for the prosecution, as well as the prisoner and a number of others called by the defence.

Opening the prosecution's case, Mr Gibson alleged that Carron had been murdered by the accused for the sake of personal gain: 'not great gain, but still personal gain', he told the jury. He went on to outline the known facts about Carron's disappearance and the events leading up to the prisoner's arrest, then dealt at length with Rowles's account of his movements between 18 and 21 May 1930, a statement which he described as 'a tissue of lies'.

Apart from the Lands Department's Chief Draughtsman, the first witness to be called on this occasion was Constable Hearn, who again gave details of his search for the victim, the finding of human remains at the rabbit reserve and the arrest of the prisoner. Hearn's evidence was very similar to that which he had given at the inquest – except that this time he said nothing about the search for Ryan and Lloyd – and Mr Curran's brief cross-examination did nothing to lessen its impact.

*

The next to appear was John Lemon, who was now a labourer in Mount Magnet. As before, he told how Carron left his outcamp in company with the prisoner on 18 May 1930, saying that he would send him some fruit and other things which the witness never received. But

128

this time he added that Carron promised to return within five weeks, as Lemon had said that he would recommend him to the Narndee manager for a job on his station.

The witness again gave details of his own search for Carron, and identified several of the objects found at Rowles's outcamp – two shirts, a wristwatch, a pair of hair-clippers and a 0.32-calibre rifle – as being similar to articles which were in Carron's possession just before he disappeared.

He also identified the torch, the open-faced watch and the camera which had been in the prisoner's utility truck as being similar to articles owned by Carron, and the gold ring found in the ashes on the rabbit reserve as the one which Carron wore on one of his little fingers. But when Mr Gibson produced the blue serge overcoat he suddenly became hesitant. 'Is that the coat I identified at the inquest at Cue?' he asked.

'Why, don't you know it?' interjected Mr Curran.

'Well, I had tried it on there,' said Lemon. 'If it is the same coat I don't see why I should put it on again. It doesn't look too clean now!'

He had no difficulty identifying the hat, however, and said that he would know it after ten years. He remembered that Carron had it with him when he left Narndee Station on the day of his disappearance, and that he (the witness) borrowed it from him in order to wear it for a photograph.

Lemon was cross-examined at greater length than Hearn, but answered most of Mr Curran's questions with an air of self-assurance. He said that after arriving in Western Australia in February 1930, he and Carron made their way from Perth to Mount Magnet by walking, getting lifts and 'jumping the rattler'. He denied that he had seen Carron drink beer on one occasion, and likewise denied the suggestion that he and his friend had tried unsuccessfully to leave the country on a wheat boat from Geraldton.

Asked when he and Carron discussed the cheque for £25 0s 7d at his outcamp, the witness replied that it was on the night of 17 May.

'Did not Rowles go out shooting that day, and return with three eagles you had poisoned?' asked Mr Curran.

'Yes,' answered Lemon.

'Was it not while he was away that the cheque was discussed?'

'No, it was that night.'

'All trappers carry poison, don't they?'

'Yes, certainly.'

'You used to carry it yourself?'

'I was never without it.'

Lemon was unable to say whether Carron had been wearing his wristwatch on the morning of 18 May, but told Mr Curran that he had seen it among his belongings at the Narndee outcamp. In answer to further questions, he admitted that Carron was careless with his belongings and used to leave them lying about in the hut. He also agreed that when Rowles camped there most of *his* gear was left out in his truck, and so must have included 'dozens of things' which the witness never saw.

When Lemon was asked how he could identify Carron's hat, which had no distinguishing marks, he could not give a reason, but insisted that he knew it. He was then asked how Carron had worn it, and put it on cocked at a rakish angle over his right eye. He kept it there while the jury compared it with what was alleged to be the same one in a photograph of Carron.

'How can you recognize Carron's ring?' asked Mr Curran. 'Did Carron ever take it off for you to examine?'

'No, he pointed out the peculiar markings on the outside. He said it was too tight to get off, and he thought of having it filed off.'

As for the overcoat which had allegedly belonged to Carron, Lemon said that putting it on helped him to identify it. 'It was the right size for me, though a little short in the sleeves,' he explained. He added, 'Every time you touch it, it rustles like a newspaper.'

On being ordered by the judge to put it on, the witness took hold of it and made it rustle. 'Hear that!' he exclaimed. 'Hear that! It's like putting your hand in a bag of peanuts!' He then tried it on, and it was seen to fit him fairly well.

After a few more questions, mainly about the way Rowles had been dressed on the morning of 18 May 1930, Mr Curran asked Lemon if he knew that Carron had come from Canada. Lemon replied that he did.

'Did he ever say he was going back?'

'No.'

Mr Curran then embarked on a line of questioning which caused much surprise:

'In January 1931, at Mount Magnet, you exchanged a car for a motorcycle, didn't you?' he asked.

'I did,' the witness replied.

'Now in February of this year you were going around a lot with a Mr Broadbent, weren't you?'

'With Bobby Broadbent? Yes.'

'Did you tell him that if you liked to open your mouth you could get Rowles out of this?'

'No — never in my life.'

'Did you not tell him that when you exchanged your car for the motorcycle Carron was with you?'

'No, I never saw Carron again after 18 May 1930,' insisted Lemon. 'It was in January 1931 that I reported his disappearance to the police.'

But having suggested that Carron was still alive eight months after the date of his alleged murder, Mr Curran concluded his cross-examination with a further attempt to undermine Lemon's credibility:

'Your correct name is not Lemon, is it?' he asked.

'What is it, then?' asked Lemon.

'I am asking you!' said Mr Curran.

'It is John James Lemon,' replied the witness.

'You did not use that name in the Eastern States?'

'Yes, I did – except at booze parties.'

Asked by the Crown Prosecutor who Broadbent was, Lemon merely said, 'I first met him in Mount Magnet, and saw him in Perth in February of this year.'

In answer to a further question, he denied that he had ever discussed Rowles in the street with anyone.

When Arthur Upfield followed Lemon into the witness-box, on the second day of the trial, Mr Curran asked the judge to note his objection to the novelist's evidence, on the ground that it was irrelevant. The judge did so.

Upfield then told the court of his employment as a boundary rider on the rabbit-proof fence, his acquaintance with the prisoner, and the discussion at the camel station homestead about how to dispose of human remains. The discussion took place while those present – Rowles among them – were sitting round a fire, he explained.

'Was any particular method suggested?' asked Mr Gibson.

'Yes,' replied Upfield.

'By whom?' asked the judge.

'By George Ritchie,' said the witness. 'The method was that the man was to be shot in the bush and then thoroughly burnt. The following day, when the ashes were cold, they were to be sieved for bones, which were to be pulverized in a dolly-pot. Any metal objects were to be disposed of in some manner.'

'You do not say Rowles joined in?' asked Mr Curran.

'Look, it was a small room and you don't think he sat there dumb all night?' Upfield retorted. 'Certainly he joined in!'

'What did he say?'

'How can I say that after two years?'

'You remember that Ritchie suggested the plot, though?'

'Yes. Ritchie had suggested it several months before.'

'Oh, so you go around the Murchison discussing plots for murder stories with the various people you meet?' asked the defence counsel.

'Yes,' replied Upfield.

'I do not see what that has to do with the case,' said Mr Justice Draper.

That was all the evidence which Upfield had to give on this occasion, and his testimony was hardly an impressive one. No doubt his apparent carelessness and ill humour were due to an attack of panic beforehand, when he suddenly realized that he could not trust his memory on points of detail.

15. Manning at Fremantle Jail

On the afternoon of the second day the witness box was occupied by Detective Sergeant Manning, most of whose evidence was of a corroborative nature. Manning described his visit to the rabbit reserve in company with Constable Hearn on 1 March 1931, and the finding there of objects which had not been discovered earlier by Hearn and McArthur.

He also told of the arrest of Snowy Rowles five days later, the search of his outcamp on Hill View Station and the statements and remarks that he allegedly made while in custody in Meekatharra.

He then concluded by saying that further inquiries had been made about Carron through the newspapers and the *Police Gazette*, and that all of them had proved fruitless.

When the trial was resumed the following morning, Manning was subjected to a searching cross-examination, during the course of which a number of serious allegations were made against him.

Mr Curran suggested that the witness had 'very prejudiced views about the accused' because Rowles had escaped from him in Dalwallinu, but Manning denied that that was so.

'You were in charge of that case?' asked the defence counsel.

'I prosecuted,' said Manning. 'He got away after I left.'

'Was Rowles in custody then?' asked the judge.

'He had been committed for sentence on a charge at Dalwallinu,' the detective explained.

'You advertised for Rowles in the *Police Gazette*, you said,' continued Mr Curran. 'Apparently the *Police Gazette* is not much good, as Rowles gave evidence after that, in June 1930, in a police court case at Mount Magnet.'

To this, the witness could only reply that the prisoner had been known as Smith when he escaped, and had given evidence under the name of Rowles.

'Those statements you put in as evidence were taken from Rowles ten months after the incidents they dealt with, weren't they?' asked Mr Curran.

'Yes, about that,' said Manning.

'He was rather upset, wasn't he?'

'No, he is a type not easily upset. He refused to answer any questions. He just made his statement in his own way and I took it down.'

'You asked him to explain his movements with Carron, didn't you?'

'I said that Carron had mysteriously disappeared and that others had told what they knew about it. Rowles then went straight ahead and told me what he knew.'

On being asked if he had questioned Rowles about Carron's cheque for £25 0s 7d, Manning replied, 'No, he mentioned that himself.'

'You wouldn't expect him to remember everything?' asked Mr Curran.

'I wouldn't like to express an opinion on that.'

'Rowles was handcuffed when you were taking down

his statement, wasn't he?'

'No, it was in an office. The police were at the door. They were taking no risks.'

'You were fond of having Rowles handcuffed, weren't you?'

'No, I had him handcuffed in the bush. I have been in the bush too much to take risks there.'

'But you were fond of having him handcuffed?' persisted Mr Curran. 'At the inquest at Cue you had him put in handcuffs and had him brought into court the first day handcuffed to a constable. You also had six policemen on guard.'

'I was not responsible for the safe custody of Rowles at Cue.'

Challenging Manning's evidence about Rowles's remark that a man 'must have a kink to do a thing like this', Mr Curran suggested that his client had really said that a man 'would *have* to have a kink'. He then made further allegations which the witness hotly denied:

'I believe you visited Rowles in the Fremantle Jail in April 1931?'

'Yes.'

'You wanted him to make another statement?'

'No.'

'Will you swear that you did not ask him to make another statement about the camera, and when he refused you said, "You'll wish to — that you were dead before I've finished with you"?'

'It is an absolute lie, and you know it!'

'You know he was placed in solitary confinement after that visit?'

'I know no such thing!'

Questioned further on the matter, Manning said that the whole story was a fabrication. He also indignantly denied a suggestion that he took tobacco and sweets to a long-term prisoner named Forrester, offering to 'make it worth his while' to make a statement on the case.

135

'I will explain the whole thing,' he said. 'There is nothing to keep back. I heard that Forrester had received a note from Rowles, written on a cigarette paper, asking Forrester to keep in touch with all press clippings relating to the case, and I went down and made inquiries.'

Asked about some documents which he had taken from the prisoner, and which Mr Curran said his client needed to see for the purposes of his defence, Manning said that he was not in charge of the exhibits. Mr Gibson then said that there were only two accounts and a letter, and that Rowles could see them if he wanted to.

When Manning was questioned about some false teeth which Rowles claimed were his own, he replied, 'We've got some broken teeth, and we are not satisfied yet that they do belong to Rowles. It was only at Cue that he said they were his.'

'Have you advertised in Canada for Carron?' asked Mr Curran.

'Not directly,' answered the witness.

'Don't you know that he is a Canadian?'

'No, I'm not certain.'

Mr Curran produced a copy of the *Police Gazette* dated 11 February 1931, in which Carron was described as a Canadian, but Manning said that he had not written the paragraph in question. There was now some doubt about whether Carron was really a Canadian or a New Zealander, he explained.

Re-examined by Mr Gibson, he said that the broken false teeth referred to had been found in a tin filled with flour at Rowles's outcamp.

16. An unskilled worker's mistake

After Manning, the prosecution called a number of witnesses to identify objects found at the rabbit reserve. The first witness was Dr W.S. McGillivray, the Government Pathologist, who informed the court that he had examined some of the articles in question and found them to be pieces of skull bone, a human molar, and roots and pieces of other teeth. He was then handed some other objects and said that they were artificial teeth.

'A human being's?' asked Mr Gibson.

'Well, kangaroos don't wear them!' remarked the judge.

As at the inquest, McGillivray said that it was impossible to state whether the pieces of skull bone were from an aboriginal or a European skull, as they were too small. However, he was followed by another pathologist, Dr McKenzie, who said that he had pieced some of the fragments together and, after comparing them with both aboriginal and European skulls, had come to the conclusion that they were from a European.

'I believe that skull bones burn more slowly than any other human bones?' asked Mr Gibson.

'That is so,' replied the witness. 'It is because the skull is protected by hair, which, when burnt, forms a protecting layer of a sulphur compound over the skull, and also because the brain provides a moist coating for the inside of the skull.'

The next witness was Arthur William Sims, the Hamilton dentist, who again identified Carron from photographs as Leslie George Brown, and told how he filled an upper molar tooth and made a complete lower denture for him, using diatoric teeth, in August 1929.

When he was asked whether Carron had any other artificial teeth, Sims replied, 'Yes, he had a partial upper denture, containing four pin teeth kept in place with two gold bands.'

He explained that diatoric teeth differed from pin teeth in that there were no pins for attaching them to the vulcanite of the plate.

Sims then examined the artificial teeth found at the rabbit reserve and said that there were almost enough diatoric teeth to make a complete lower denture and four pin teeth from an upper denture. He added that fire was unlikely to damage the artificial teeth, but that the vulcanite would burn. As for the amalgam filling in a tooth, that would be destroyed by heat, he said.

Looking through a pile of burnt human teeth which had been recovered from the piles of ashes, the witness selected an upper molar which he said had been filled on the biting surface, as Carron's was. He said that he believed it to be a European's tooth rather than an aboriginal's.

'You have never dealt with Australian aborigines' teeth in New Zealand, have you?' asked the judge.

'No, but since I have been here I have examined over five hundred teeth of aborigines. I have found that aborigines' teeth are generally better formed, more regular, larger and in better condition that Europeans' teeth. I never saw an aboriginal with an upper molar as small as the one produced.'

In answer to questions from the defence, Sims said that he only knew Carron slightly – though Carron had a shop where he was accustomed to making purchases – but could still remember his teeth. 'It is usual to find a complete artificial upper denture and a partial artificial lower denture in one mouth, but not the other way about,' he explained.

When Sims left the witness-box, Carron's widow, Minnie Alice Brown, was called. She gave evidence about her unhappy marriage, her husband's teeth and the purchasing of her wedding ring, identifying the ring found at the rabbit reserve as hers and other articles as her husband's property or as being similar to articles which he had owned.

In answer to a question from the judge about her husband's occupation, she said that in New Zealand he drove a baker's delivery van and also ran a mixed business.

When Mr Curran suggested that she could not really be sure that the ring was hers, Mrs Brown claimed that she could. She said that she could recognize it by a mark left where it had been cut down to fit her finger, and by other marks on the inside to which her husband had drawn her attention. These marks, together with the ring's general appearance, were sufficient to convince her that it was her own.

Mrs Brown was then asked if she knew that her husband was a Canadian.

'My husband sometimes said he was, but on our marriage certificate he gave Gisborne, New Zealand, as his birthplace,' she replied.

'But you knew he was born in Canada?' asked Mr Curran.

'I knew he was born in Gisborne,' said the witness.

This was the opposite of what she had said at the inquest, but Mr Curran did not ask her to account for this discrepancy. Instead, he read extracts from a letter which Carron had written to a sister in New Zealand in March 1930, arguing that they were proof that he intended going back to Canada. Mrs Brown could only say that she did not know of any such intention on her husband's part.

However, when the defence suggested that the same letter showed Carron to have had beer bought for him on one occasion, her denial was more positive. 'My husband didn't drink,' she declared.

When Mrs Brown's cross-examination was finished, Sims the dentist made a brief reappearance. This time he produced his record of the work which he had done for Carron and explained the entries to the defence. He also examined the gold clips found at the rabbit reserve and said that they were similar to the ones which Carron had had in his upper denture.

The next witness, Graham Poocke, was the Superintendent of the Perth Dental Hospital. He merely corroborated Sims's evidence regarding the artificial teeth which had been found and, with some difficulty, identified the two pieces of the upper molar which had been filled.

The last of this group of witnesses was Andrew Thomas Long, the Auckland jeweller. Long examined the wedding ring, which he had been unable to identify positively at the inquest, and this time said that it was the one he had sold to Mrs Brown, and cut down to fit her finger, in December 1925.

Questioned by Mr Curran, he agreed that during the course of a single year many such wedding rings were sold in New Zealand. But on being recalled the following day, after several other witnesses had given evidence, he revealed that the cutting-down had been done by an unskilled worker, who used 15-carat instead of 18-carat gold solder.

At this point the ring was shown to the jury, so that each member could see for himself how clearly the join showed up.

*

When Long left the witness-box the first time, on the afternoon of the third day, Alice Jones, the hotel proprietor's daughter from Youanmi, made a brief appearance. As at the inquest, she identified a photograph which Rowles had given her of himself and said that it was the only one that he had ever given her. She believed that it had been taken by Maddison.

John Worth, the former bookkeeper at Wydgee Station, also appeared briefly. He identified the cheque for £25 0s 7d with which Carron had been paid off when he left the station and said that he remembered Carron's two watches being returned by Levinson and Sons, to whom they had been sent for repair.

The prosecution then called the first of a number of

140

witnesses to give evidence about Rowles's movements after he left Narndee Station with Carron on the morning of 18 May 1930.

17. A trip to Youanmi

In his own statement to Detective Sergeant Manning, Rowles claimed that he and Carron drove eastwards from Lemon's outcamp to the No. 1 Rabbit-Proof Fence, then northwards to Windimurra Station, where they camped in an old unoccupied homestead and set traps for foxes nearby.

The following day, 19 May, he went into Paynesville to buy stores and stayed the night at the Paynesville Hotel while Carron remained at the homestead on his own, the statement continued.

Rowles then returned to the homestead on the morning of 20 May, and stayed with Carron until the evening of 21 May, when they went into Mount Magnet together, had supper at a shop run by a couple named Slavin, and parted company shortly afterwards.

But prosecution evidence produced at this stage of the trial showed that Rowles arrived at the Paynesville Hotel on 20 May – a day later than in his own account – left about 10 a.m. on 21 May, and turned up in Youanmi, sixty-three miles away, about noon the same day.

It also showed that there was nobody at the old Windimurra homestead when Rowles said that he and Carron were camping there, and that there was no truth in his story about them having supper at the shop run by the Slavins either.

*

The first of this group of witnesses was Edward Samuel Moses, the Paynesville Hotel proprietor, who told the court that Rowles arrived at his hotel on 20 May, claiming to have come from Narndee Station. He stayed the night there, bought goods from the hotel store – including sixteen gallons of petrol – and got the witness to cash Carron's cheque for him after endorsing it with Carron's name himself.

Moses went on to say that before he left the hotel the following morning the prisoner took about six bottles of Globe beer from him – which was rather more than the 'couple of bottles' which the same witness had mentioned at the inquest – saying that he wanted to take a drink back to the fox-traps for Carron. The witness also said that he had never bought any pelts or scalps from the prisoner in his life.

'How can you remember that you gave Rowles Globe beer?' Mr Curran asked him. 'It was two years ago.'

'I was short of beer at the time,' replied Moses. 'There were only seven bottles in the place.'

'Did you notice any change in Rowles's appearance on that occasion?'

'No, he appeared to be as usual.'

'When you say Rowles left your hotel at 10 a.m. you are only guessing, aren't you?'

'I was only guessing at Cue, but I can say now it was 10 a.m. or shortly afterwards. I remember asking Rowles to have a cup of morning tea before he left.'

Moses was followed by James Henry Jones, who said that Rowles booked into his hotel in Youanmi on 21 May, having arrived there in his utility truck. He gave the witness Moses's cheque for £17 to change, taking £1 in cash to be going on with and the rest in drinks and subsequent cash payments. He told Jones that he had received the cheque in payment for some fox or dingo scalps.

The witness admitted that he could not say with certainty that Rowles had slept at the hotel on the night of 21 May, but said his books showed him as having had full board and lodging from that date until 2 June.

'But he was continually coming and going from Youanmi on his trapping expeditions, wasn't he?' asked Mr Curran.

'On other occasions that he stayed with me he was, but I do not know about the period between 21 May and 2 June 1930,' replied Jones. 'He is shown in my books as having had full board and lodging for that period.'

'I understand that he had a room at your hotel where he could leave his trapping gear when he was absent?'

'Yes, he used to leave his traps there, but I would not book him up for the full period while he was absent.'

Asked by the judge how far the rabbit reserve was from Youanmi, the witness replied that it was roughly forty-one miles. On the question of keeping Globe beer at his hotel, he said that he only did so on a few occasions, and that he always got it in Paynesville.

Mr Curran produced Rowles's hotel bill and asked Jones to account for a charge for tea on 22 May. This threw him into confusion, as it appeared to suggest that Rowles had had his first meal there on that date rather than the day before, and the witness could only say that the item must have been wrongly dated or that it applied to a meal for somebody visiting Rowles.

In answer to further questions from the defence, Jones agreed that Rowles, who had worked for him after leaving Challi Bore in December 1929, was a good, reliable worker, and that he had been in credit at the hotel when he left to take up a job somewhere else.

Thomas Jay, the husband of the postmistress, again told of Rowles's arrival in Youanmi on 21 May 1930. He said that Rowles called at the post office about noon, and took the witness and his wife out to deliver a telegram to a man named O'Connor. When they got back to Youanmi, he went over to Jones's hotel, then returned to the post office, where he drank the last of several bottles of Globe beer on his own.

When Jay refused to accept that he might have been

mistaken about what had happened, Mr Curran suggested that he may have been 'not very well disposed towards Rowles'. Jay denied this, but had to admit that he and Rowles had once come to blows over an accusation that Rowles had killed his dog. He was then asked whether on that occasion Rowles had put him in bed for a couple of days.

'Put me in bed?' he asked indignantly. 'I might have put *him* in bed if I had gone on with the fight!'

Another witness called to discredit the prisoner's statement was Albert Leonard Wilkins, the overseer on Windimurra Station, who said that there was no truth in the story about Rowles and Carron camping in the old Windimurra homestead after leaving Narndee, and that he had heard no shots fired in the vicinity on the days that Rowles had said they were hunting there.

Wilkins was followed by Drefus Callum Grieve, a yardman on the same station, who denied a claim that Rowles had seen and waved to him on arrival at Windimurra on 18 May.

Catherine Slavin, who said that she and her husband kept a fruit and confectionery shop in Mount Magnet, where they also served light meals, was equally sure that Rowles and Carron did *not* have supper there on the evening of 21 May.

Mrs Slavin told the court that Carron only ever visited her shop once; that was on a Sunday morning in February 1930, when he had breakfast there with John Lemon. She also said that Rowles appeared there several times, and once had supper there with 'Tip' Jones, the hotel proprietor's son.

'Are you sure it was Tip Jones?' asked Mr Curran. 'I am instructed it was not Tip Jones.'

'Yes, it was,' the witness insisted.

Mr Curran then asked her whether she knew a man named O'Dea. 'Yes,' she answered.

'Well, I am instructed that Rowles came into your

shop with Carron, and O'Dea came in and spoke to them,' said Mr Curran. 'Carron went out first, and as Rowles went out you asked O'Dea who he was. O'Dea told you it was Snowy Rowles. Do you remember that?'

'I do not,' replied Mrs Slavin.

18. A rifle from Wydgee Station

After Mrs Slavin, several witnesses were called to give evidence about articles which had been in the prisoner's possession at the time of his arrest, or objects found at the rabbit reserve. Among these witnesses were Frederick John Wimbridge, the part-owner of Hill View Station; John Joseph Wheelock, the former stockman; Ian Thom, the new Wydgee Station manager, and Lancelot Bowen Maddison, the boundary rider.

Wimbridge, who had not been called at the inquest, said that Rowles started working at Hill View on 29 November 1930. He was stationed at the Hill View outcamp, a one-roomed hut where various articles belonging to the station, including a 0.32-calibre rifle and an old double-barrelled shotgun, had been left.

Before going out to the outcamp, Rowles left certain articles of his own at the station shearing sheds, and these were taken to Meekatharra Police Station after his arrest, the witness told the court. The overcoat which John Lemon and Mrs Brown had identified as Carron's was among them.

Under cross-examination, Wimbridge agreed that the prisoner had not been alone all the time he was at the outcamp, as a native named Brumby stayed and worked with him for about six weeks. He also admitted that he had not seen Rowles leave his belongings at the shearing sheds, but said Rowles had told him that they were there.

Wheelock, who was now a prospector, said that he was working on Wydgee Station at the same time as

Carron, and that it was at his outcamp that Rowles and Carron met on 15 May 1930, and stayed the night before going to Lemon's outcamp on Narndee. He identified the hair-clippers as being similar to those which Carron had owned.

'When Carron arrived, did he have his belongings with him?' asked Mr Gibson.

'He had his swag, but later that day he went back to the Wydgee Station homestead with Rowles in Rowles's truck to get the remainder of his belongings,' replied the witness.

'Did he have any firearms when he returned?'

'Yes, Carron had a 0.32-calibre Winchester rifle, belonging to the Wydgee Pastoral Company. They arrived back between eight o'clock and nine o'clock that night.'

'Did Carron do anything to the rifle?'

'He tried to put a foresight on it, using a small coin for the purpose, but he could not finish the job because he did not have the necessary tools.'

Cross-examined, Wheelock said Carron had told him that he was taking the rifle, even though it did not belong to him.

'Rowles gave you a 0.32 Winchester before he left, didn't he?' Mr Curran then asked.

'Yes,' said Wheelock. 'But that was not the rifle Carron took away with him.'

Thom told the court that he knew Carron and had frequently camped with him while he was employed at Wydgee Station. He knew that Carron wore a gold ring on the little finger of his right hand, and had seen him with a pair of clippers. He had also seen him with a torch, but on being shown the one found in Rowles's truck, he said he did not think that that was the one.

'Did Carron have a 0.32-calibre Winchester rifle in his possession at Wydgee Station?' asked Mr Gibson.

'Yes, it was a very old one,' said the witness. 'It was

station property.'

'Did Carron take it away with him when he left the station?'

'Yes.'

'He made no secret of taking it?'

'No.'

Thom said that the rifle found at Rowles's outcamp was very similar to the one Carron had taken, and that the French coffee tin found at the rabbit reserve was very similar to one in which Carron had kept his shaving things. He then identified the white-handled razor which had been in the parcel at Hill View outcamp, saying that it had rust marks which he recognized, as well as having the word 'Puma' marked on its blade and the name of a New Zealand firm engraved on it. When questioned by Mr Curran, however, Thom had to admit that he had not identified this exhibit so positively when he gave evidence at the inquest.

Maddison gave his evidence about camping with Rowles near the 183-mile gate. He told of his visit to the Hill View outcamp in company with Mrs Annie Brown and her son, and of the finding of a camera in the prisoner's utility truck. He also told how Rowles had given him a Borsalino hat in exchange for a cap.

Maddison was questioned by both Mr Gibson and Mr Curran about the state of the hut on the rabbit reserve, and explained that it was unfit for camping in because galahs and kangaroos had been inside it.

'Have you ever known of anybody camping in the hut while you have been boundary riding on the rabbit-proof fence?' asked Mr Curran.

'I saw signs that someone had camped there on one occasion only, and that was about eighteen months ago,' he replied.

'You once camped with Rowles at Yandil, near Meekatharra, I believe?' Mr Curran then asked.

'Yes,' the witness agreed.

'You had a hundred and twenty pounds with you then?'

'I did.'

'Rowles knew you had it, didn't he?'

'Yes.'

Replying to further questions from Mr Curran, the witness said that he had never seen Rowles wearing a grey suit in the bush – as Lemon claimed that he *had* been when he left Narndee with Carron – and that he generally wore moleskins, elastic-sided boots and overalls.

Annie Mary Brown corroborated Maddison's account of the discovery of the camera in Rowles's truck. Cross-examined, she said that she had, at the prisoner's request, bought a tyre for the truck, and that Rowles still owed her £2 for it. It was after she had bought the tyre that the camera was found.

'Didn't you buy Rowles a shaving outfit for a Christmas present in 1930?' asked Mr Curran.

'No,' replied the witness.

Albert Robert Bates, a station hand, said that between June and October 1930 he occupied the outcamp on Hill View Station where Rowles was later found. When he left there was a 0.32-calibre Winchester rifle and a shotgun in the camp, and both of these, as far as he knew, belonged to the station. He had sawn the end off the rifle because it was shooting low, he added.

Asked about the shelf in the outcamp, Bates said that he knew there was one but that he had not left a parcel on it. He had twice looked on this shelf for nails, etc., but had not seen a parcel there, he told Mr Curran.

*

Although Rowles was only on trial for Carron's murder, four witnesses were called to give evidence concerning the disappearance of James Ryan and George Lloyd.

First, Charles Bogle, the station manager at Narndee, told how the two men apparently left Challi Bore without warning between 8 and 10 December 1929, leaving the fencing of the site unfinished.

Then James Yates, the prospector, gave an account of his meeting with the prisoner at Watson's Gate, when Rowles had Ryan's utility truck with him.

Peter Morrissey, the part-owner of Anketell Station, followed, to repeat his evidence about Rowles burning something on a fire in the bush and the discovery of saucepans, enamel plates and other articles under a nearby tree some months afterwards.

Finally, William Henry Wright, the assayer, identified the saucepans referred to by the previous witness, and the camp-oven and saucepan found on the rabbit reserve, as being similar to articles owned by James Ryan.

*

After Wright had been heard, there was more police evidence. Constable Thomas Penn corroborated Manning's account of Rowles's arrest, and gave evidence about his alleged suicide attempts and self-incriminating remarks. He added that on 22 April 1931, he and Constable Fawcett received a petrol case full of goods brought into the Meekatharra lock-up by Frederick Wimbridge. Its contents included the overcoat identified as Carron's.

Cross-examined, the witness agreed that Rowles had at first been held only on a charge of escaping from custody, and that it was not until some months later that the murder charge was brought against him. He was then questioned about the prisoner's alleged suicide attempts:

'When you went into his cell on 9 March and found him with a rope made of blanket strips around his neck, don't you think he was trying to escape?'

'No.'

'Was not his truck just outside the cell?'

'He could not escape that way. We were keeping too strict a watch for that.'

'So you were watching him carefully, and yet you say that he took an overdose of strychnine the night before and you never heard anything?'

'He asked Constable Fawcett for an Aspro, saying he had a splitting headache that night.'

'And you did not consider that he was in need of a doctor, after having taken all that strychnine?'

'He did not say anything about strychnine then.'

'But was he not ill or anything?'

'He said that he had a headache.'

'Have you any knowledge of strychnine poisoning?'

'No.'

'Where did you say he had the strychnine?'

'He said he had had it in the band of his trousers.'

'Was it in any special place?'

'No, he pointed out a split in the band and said that the strychnine had been there.'

'Would it not have fallen out if he had it in such a place?'

'No.'

Re-examined, Penn said that although Rowles had not been charged with murder while he was in Meekatharra, he knew about the discovery of the ashes in the rabbit reserve, having read about it in a newspaper.

Fawcett followed Penn into the witness-box and corroborated his account of the incident in Rowles's cell. He added that Rowles asked him not to report what had occurred 'down below', and that he replied that he would have to.

Constable Penn's wife also made a brief appearance, as it was she who had been handed the petrol case full of goods by Wimbridge on 22 April 1931. When she had finished her testimony, Mr Gibson announced that that was all the evidence he intended to produce.

19. Some changes to the prisoner's story

Outlining the case for the defence on the sixth day of the trial, Mr Curran said that far from being 'a tissue of lies', the prisoner's statement to Detective Sergeant Manning about his movements in company with Louis Carron on and after 18 May 1930 had been substantially correct, and that the evidence Rowles would give would follow closely along the lines of it.

He contended that Carron had still been alive some time after Rowles was alleged to have murdered him, and that Mrs Slavin had been mistaken in saying that Rowles and Carron had never had supper together in her shop. He would produce evidence to show that she had mistaken Carron for Tip Jones, he said.

He also told the jury that he intended to produce medical evidence to confound the statements of the constables who said that Rowles had taken strychnine and only suffered a severe headache.

The prisoner then left the dock and entered the witness-box. He answered all the questions put to him calmly and without hesitation, except when complaining that the prosecution had kept certain documents of his, and carefully explained any matters relating to bush life which might otherwise not have been understood.

His real name, he agreed, was John Thomas Smith. He had been using the name Rowles since the middle of 1928, when he escaped from jail in Dalwallinu.

'Since then you have been in the Murchison?' asked Mr Curran.

'I have worked at Narndee, Hill View and Youno Downs Stations, and at Youanmi,' replied the accused.

'You have always got good wages?'

'The only time I was out of work I was trapping or prospecting.'

'Were you ever short of money?'

'Only in July or August 1930, when I was prospecting.'

'When you were trapping, did you make good money?'

'Yes.'

'How much were pelts worth then?'

'Two pounds a head.'

'How many would you get at a time?'

'Once I got seven in one night, but that was exceptional. I averaged three or four a week.'

'Did you ever run a bank account?'

'No.'

Asked about the circumstances in which he met Carron three days before they left Narndee Station together, Rowles replied, 'I had been over at Lemon's outcamp and Lemon told me that Carron was coming from Condon outcamp (on Wydgee Station) to see him, and would be carrying his swag nine miles. I said I would go over and get him. Lemon had said he would make a good mate for me.'

'Who was at Condon when you got there?' asked Mr Curran.

'Jack Wheelock,' said Rowles. 'Carron came later with Mr Beasley, manager of Wydgee Station.'

'Did he have a swag with him?'

'Yes.'

'Did you have any conversation with him?'

'Yes. He decided to come trapping and prospecting with me up towards Wiluna.'

'What happened after that?'

'We went across to Wydgee homestead, about thirty-five miles away, and got the remainder of his things. I don't know what they were – clothes and things, I think.'

'Was there a rifle?'

'Yes, he brought a rifle.'

'I believe you stayed with Wheelock that night?'

'Yes, I think it was next day we went across to Lemon's camp, and stayed there about two days.'

The prisoner denied hearing Carron discuss his

cheque with Lemon, and said that during the days they stayed at the outcamp he was out shooting most of the time. On being asked about their movements on 18 May, he again said that he and Carron drove eastwards to the rabbit-proof fence, then northwards to the 206-mile gate, where the road from Mount Magnet to Youanmi passed through it. He went on to say that they then stopped to do some shooting in the area and afterwards drove to Windimurra Station.

Rowles repeated his claim that he had seen and waved to a man working on that station. But instead of saying that he and Carron camped in the old homestead, as he had done in his statement to Manning, he told the court that they camped two or three hundred yards to the south-west of it. After making camp, they went out hunting for a while, he said.

'Did you go into Paynesville the next day?' asked Mr Curran.

'Yes,' he replied.

'What for?'

'To get some cartridges and other goods.'

'Did Carron give you a cheque to cash for him?'

'Yes.'

'When?' asked the judge.

'When he came and opened a gate for me.'

'Was it endorsed?' asked Mr Curran.

'Carron said he was going to fix it up, but there was no ink available, so Carron asked me to endorse it,' answered the accused.

Continuing his evidence, Rowles said that he arrived at Paynesville about noon and saw Mrs Moses at the hotel. He then went to see Ted Moses at the mine which he was working, about four miles away, and after a while returned to the hotel alone. When Moses arrived back, the witness arranged to get the goods he wanted, but decided to stay the night there, as he was having some trouble with his truck. He spent the evening drinking in the bar and listening to the wireless.

'You got your goods all right next day, didn't you?' asked Mr Curran.

'Yes,' he said.

'There was a prospector's dish among the goods, wasn't there?'

'Yes.'

'You had no intention of going into Youanmi to work then?'

'No.'

Asked what time he left the hotel, Rowles replied, 'It's so long ago I cannot remember. I take it that it would be about 9 a.m., as we would have breakfast about 8 a.m., and it would not take long to get the goods together and fix the valves on the truck.'

'Did you take any beer with you?'

'Yes, I took a couple of bottles in case Carron wanted a drink. Moses gave me two bottles and I bought some. I didn't know then that Carron was almost a teetotaller. I cannot remember what brand of beer I took. If Mr Moses says it was Globe brand, I take it he is right.'

'How long did it take you to get back to Windimurra?'

'About half an hour.'

'Was Carron at the camp?'

'No. He was out at the traps.'

'I believe he would have to be out early?'

'Yes. The traps would be baited with butter-baits, and he would have to get out to them before the crows got at them.'

'What time did he come back?'

'Between 11 a.m. and noon, I think.'

Rowles was then asked what happened when Carron returned, and said that he gave him some of the change from his cheque for £25 0s 7d, including the cheque Moses had given him for £17 – not £16, as in his original statement – made payable to 'S. Rowles or bearer'. 'I deducted half the cost of the goods I had bought, as

Carron had agreed to share expenses,' he added.

'Did you drink any of the beer?' asked Mr Curran.

'Yes, we drank one bottle. Carron had one glass.'

'Mr Moses said that when he asked you where you had come from, you replied, "From Narndee Station".'

'Yes, I meant I had come from that direction.'

Although in his statement to Manning he had not mentioned his visit to Youanmi, Rowles now said in answer to another question from Mr Curran that after returning to Windimurra from Paynesville he went into that town to get his prospecting tools, as he and his companion had decided to do 'a little independent prospecting'.

'Where were they?' he was asked.

'At Jones's store at Youanmi,' he answered. 'I had a lot of tools there.'

'Do you remember meeting Jay at Youanmi?'

'Yes.'

'About what time was that?'

'About 1 p.m. I cannot be sure.'

Asked the distance from Youanmi to Windimurra, he said that it was about thirty-five miles. He was then asked how long it would take him to do the journey, and replied that he could do it comfortably in an hour. His truck could do between forty-five and fifty miles an hour, he said.

At this point, a dispute took place between Mr Curran and Mr Gibson about whether Rowles's truck, which had been left in Cue, should be brought to Perth, but the question was left undecided. The prisoner then resumed his testimony, telling how he took Jay to O'Connor's place to deliver a telegram, and later went to Jones's hotel. He denied booking into the hotel, claiming that he only went there to get his prospecting tools and then went back to Windimurra.

When Mr Curran asked him why his statement to Detective Sergeant Manning contained no reference to his trip to Youanmi, Rowles replied, 'Because when I started to tell Manning about it he said he wanted to know if I had stayed at Windimurra when I returned from Paynesville, and added that he only wanted to know my movements in company with Carron.'

20. A series of denials

In answer to further questions from Mr Curran, the accused said that following his trip to Youanmi he spent another night at Windimurra with Carron. The next day they set out together in the direction of Mount Magnet, stopped on the way to do some more shooting, and arrived in the town about 10 p.m.

'What did you do there?' asked Mr Curran.

'We went into Slavin's shop and had supper.'

'Did anyone join you?'

'A man named O'Dea, who had purchased my old motor car, came in, and I introduced him to Carron,' said Rowles. 'When we had finished supper, Carron got up and went out to the truck for a handkerchief or something. I paid and then went down the street and had some drinks at the hotel. I then remembered that I had not turned off the petrol on the truck, and that the carburettor was probably flooding. I returned to the truck and was attending to the petrol tap when someone called out, "Hallo, Snow!"

'I looked up and saw Carron, who told me that he thought he would leave me, as one boozer was enough in the party. He added that he supposed I had been drinking that night, and I replied, "Well, what about that?" He said, "I suppose that's why you stayed at Paynesville that night?" – and I replied, "What of it?" He then said that he thought he would get out, as he reckoned he could do better on his own.'

'What happened then?'

'He took his swag off the truck.'

'Where did you go?'

'I went to Rodan's hotel, where I had some more drinks. While I was at the hotel Carron came up to me and asked me to cash Moses's cheque for £17, as it was made out to me, and he thought he would have difficulty in cashing it. I tried to get the barmaid at the hotel to change it, but she would not, so I cashed it for him. There were two fivers among the £17 I gave him. I did not take the numbers.'

'Where did you go after that?'

'I went back towards Youanmi. I slept on the road that night and arrived at Jones's hotel before breakfast that morning. I had breakfast at the hotel.'

'When did you give Jones the cheque for £17?'

'That day.'

The prisoner produced documents which he offered as proof that Jones had never credited him with the cheque for £17. He claimed that Jones was frequently out in his books and that there had been several disputes between them over the state of Rowles's account. If the books showed that Jones received the cheque on 21 May, then the books were wrong, he said.

He went on to repeat his claim that he had later received a letter and a photograph from Carron, but could not produce either of them or give a satisfactory reason for not being able to do so.

On being questioned about his arrest at the Hill View outcamp, he agreed that he had asked Manning if he could change his clothes, saying that he had been 'knocking around working on the windmills' and was very dirty. But he denied having strychnine hidden in his trousers, and challenged the prosecution to produce them and show the court where it had been hidden. As for whether he had swallowed the poison while in police custody in Meekatharra, he dismissed the allegation by saying, 'If I had done so, I would not be sitting here.'

He likewise denied trying to hang himself, telling Mr

Curran that he had fallen heavily while climbing his improvised rope in an attempt to escape. He claimed that he had simulated an unsuccessful suicide attempt in order to hide his real intention.

'Have you ever tried to commit suicide?' asked Mr Curran.

'Never,' replied Rowles.

'Have you had any opportunities?'

'Plenty. When I was lodged in Fremantle Jail, I was put in the bootmakers' shop, where I had the handling of knives. After Detective Sergeant Manning visited the jail I was taken out of the shop and segregated. That meant I was kept on my own for twenty-two and a half hours a day.'

'You have been shaving yourself at the Fremantle Jail, I believe?'

'I have been using a blade-razor ever since I have been there. I have got it hidden in my cell, and will produce it if necessary.'

Rowles further denied making the self-incriminating remarks attributed to him by Manning and Penn, and then gave his own account of how articles which were believed to be Carron's property had come to be in his possession.

The Borsalino hat which he had given to Maddison in exchange for a cap had, he said, been sold to him by a hawker named Coas on Yoweragabbie Station; the camera found in his truck had been sent to him by his brother for a birthday present in August or September 1930; the hair-clippers he had bought from Sher Ali, the Afghan, for 12s 6d in April 1930; the torch he had bought from a man named Maloney in Meekatharra towards the end of 1930; a pocket-knife worn on his belt at the time of his arrest had been given to him by Maddison, and the sheath which it was in had been among station property which he found at his outcamp on Hill View.

'What about the overcoat?' asked Mr Curran.

'I never saw it before it was produced at Cue,' replied the prisoner. 'Carron left some of his goods in the petrol cases on my truck when he parted from me at Mount Magnet. I later took them, along with the petrol cases containing my gear, to Hill View Station. Some of the cases were left at the station outcamp and some at the shearers' quarters. The coat might have been left in one of the cases, but I don't think it could have been or I would have seen it. Is it likely that I would have kept it, knowing the police were inquiring for this man?'

'What about the 0.32 Winchester rifle? You told the police that it did not belong to you.'

'I knew that it belonged to the Wydgee Pastoral Company, and that Carron had stolen it. I was not going to claim it. Carron left it on the truck. I didn't want it. I had given John Wheelock a rifle of the same pattern the day Carron joined me.'

The prisoner was then asked about the Omega openfaced watch set in the dashboard of his truck. In his statement to Manning he had said that it was already there when he bought the vehicle from Ryan in December 1929, but as jewellers' markings had since shown that it was one of the watches owned by Carron, he was obviously obliged to explain the matter. He did so readily.

'Carron must have changed his watch for the one in the holder in the dashboard of my truck,' he said. 'I remember when we were together that Carron broke the watch-glass in his own watch, and I gave him a leather holder to protect the face of the damaged watch. Without my knowledge, Carron must have exchanged the two watches. I never noticed that the exchange had been made, as I had never inspected the original watch in the truck dashboard.'

'When did you discover the watch was not yours?' asked the judge.

'At the inquest, when evidence concerning the markings on it showed that it was Carron's.'

Rowles had then to explain the parcel found on the shelf at his outcamp – but did so without apparent difficulty. 'Carron must have left the parcel in one of the petrol cases that I later placed in the outcamp at Hill View Station,' he said. 'When I was breaking in a chestnut horse for Mr Wimbridge later in 1930, I sent the native Brumby, who was working for me then, to the outcamp to get a petrol case which I wanted for a feed box for the horse. He got the box and must have thrown its contents up onto the shelf where they were found.'

21. Supper in Mount Magnet

Under cross-examination, Rowles continued to answer as readily as before. He was obviously aware that some parts of his story contradicted the evidence of his statement to Manning, but seemed not to be unduly concerned about this. He evidently thought that it could be satisfactorily explained, like everything else in the prosecution's case.

'Which print was it that Carron sent you from Geraldton?' asked Mr Gibson.

'One of me standing by my truck,' replied Rowles. 'It was on a spool Carron took with him in his camera.'

'Where is it?'

'Among my belongings.'

'But you have all your snaps in your pocket now. Do you suggest that the Crown has deliberately kept some of them?'

'Certainly, I do. They have kept a book of mine, too.'

'And what about the letter Carron sent you with the snap?'

'That should be among my belongings, too.'

'But in your statement you said you did not know where it was.'

'That's how Manning wrote it down. I told him the letter was in my belongings. He said it was not, and I told him that if it was not, I did not know where it was. I could not look for it. I was handcuffed at one end of the table, and Manning was writing at the other end of the table.'

When Mr Gibson asked him how long he had spent hunting at Windimurra before going into Paynesville, the prisoner said that he may have been mistaken when he told Manning that it was only one day. If he left Lemon's outcamp on 18 May and arrived in Paynesville on 20 May, as alleged, he must have spent two days hunting with Carron, he continued. He added that he was taking the Crown's word for it that he left Lemon's camp on 18 May.

On the subject of his visit to Youanmi, Rowles again said that he did not stay there on 21 May, and claimed that he left to go back to Windimurra about 6 p.m. He denied having been a guest at the Youanmi Hotel on 22 May, saying that he was not there that day, and said that the receipted bill for tea which had been produced earlier in the trial was wrong. He likewise denied buying overalls at Jones's store on that date, saying that a sale booked to him in Jones's docket book on 22 May must have been wrongly dated.

'You say that O'Dea met you while you were having supper with Carron on 22 May at Mount Magnet,' Mr Gibson persisted. 'Why didn't you mention that to Detective Sergeant Manning when he asked you if you could name anyone who had seen you with Carron?'

'I didn't think it important,' replied Rowles.

'You realize it is important now, though?'

'I thought that you would have found out your mistake about me long before this!'

Returning to the subject of the letter which he claimed to have received from Carron after they had parted company, Mr Gibson asked Rowles how he accounted for Carron writing to him but not to Lemon, who was his best friend. Rowles brushed the question aside by saying that he did not have to account for it.

'Did Carron say anything in his letter about having left some of his things in your truck?' asked Mr Gibson.

'No,' replied the prisoner. 'I would have known they were there if he had mentioned them.'

'When you wrote to Lemon, following his telegram inquiring for Carron, you told Lemon that Carron had gone to Geraldton and had promised to send some snaps, but had not done so,' the prosecutor continued. 'Yet you told Detective Sergeant Manning that Carron had sent you a snapshot with the letter.'

'That snapshot was for me, not for Lemon,' replied Rowles.

In answer to further questions, the prisoner agreed that he had not called on Lemon since leaving his camp in May 1930, though he had been up and down the rabbit-proof fence. Asked why that was, he replied, 'Well, I was not near his camp, and I was not going to travel ten or twenty miles across country just to see him.'

With this, the cross-examination was concluded. But before leaving the witness-box, Rowles, at the request of the foreman of the jury, put on the Borsalino hat which had been identified as Carron's. It was seen to fit him well.

22. An attempt to discredit John Lemon

The defence then produced its medical evidence to refute the allegation that Rowles had tried to poison himself with strychnine in the Meekatharra lock-up. Dr D. McKenzie, of Perth – the second Dr McKenzie to appear at this trial – told the court that strychnine was one of the most potent of all poisons, and that only a small quantity of it was needed to cause death. Victims of this type of poisoning suffered muscular spasms and died in agony within a short time if they were not treated, he continued. Had Rowles taken strychnine, there would certainly have been noticeable effects afterwards.

Dr McKenzie was followed by Robert Broadbent, a prospector of Mount Magnet, who had been mentioned during the cross-examination of John Lemon. Broadbent testified that he had met Lemon in Mount Magnet two years previously, and that he had seen a lot of him while on a recent holiday in Perth. He said that before leaving for the inquest at Cue, Lemon told him that for £200 he could get Rowles out of trouble, as Carron had been present when he exchanged his car for a motorcycle in January 1931.

During the course of his testimony, Broadbent claimed that he and Lemon had talked about the subject twice, both times in Perth. The first time was on the Monday before the inquest started, the second two or three days later. When the prosecutor pointed out that Lemon had left for Cue, over 500 miles away, on the Monday before the inquest, Broadbent could only say that he knew that and insist that he was speaking the truth. He then had to admit that he had a police record.

George William Smith, of north Perth, the brother of the accused, appeared next. He told the court that in August 1930 he sent the prisoner a parcel for his birthday, containing a birthday cake, some clothes and a camera similar to the one produced. Unfortunately for the defence, he had no record of it.

After Smith, Julian O'Dea, of Mount Magnet, was called. This witness said that from the beginning of 1930 to the middle of 1931 he was employed driving the mail-coach from Yoweragabbie to Narndee Station, and knew both Carron and the accused. One night about the middle of 1930 he saw the two men having supper together in the shop run by the Slavins in Mount Magnet and went to join them, he told Mr Curran. He said he knew that this was after Carron had left Wydgee Station, because he remembered him saying that he had left.

'When did you first make a statement about this meeting?' asked Mr Gibson.

'When Mr Curran interviewed me,' said O'Dea.

'Was that after the Cue inquest?'

'Yes.'

Asked why he had not told the police that he had seen Carron alive after the date of his alleged murder, O'Dea replied, 'I am not a man who likes to push himself forward, and I considered the less I had to do with the case the better.'

'If Mr Curran had not taken a statement from you, you would have remained silent then?' asked the prosecutor.

'Yes,' said the witness.

Harold Jones, known as Tip Jones, the hotel proprietor's son, also appeared as a defence witness, denying that he had ever had supper with Rowles in Slavin's shop, as Catherine Slavin had claimed.

After that, John Lemon was recalled, to give evidence rebutting that of Broadbent. He agreed that he had seen Broadbent just before catching the train to Cue for the inquest, but said that he did not say more than a few words to him. 'In fact,' he added, 'Broadbent did not have time to put the nips in for two shillings, as was his practice.'

'Will you swear that you did not have various conversations with Broadbent early this year?' asked Mr Curran.

'I did speak with him at various hotels around Perth, but I never discussed the case with him,' replied Lemon.

In answer to a further question, however, the witness admitted that when he arrived in Western Australia he was not travelling under the name of Lemon.

Detective Sergeant Manning was then recalled, to answer questions arising out of the prisoner's own evidence. He said that when Rowles made his statement about his movements in company with Carron, he made no mention of his trip to Youanmi.

'Did you ask him if he could name anyone who saw him with Carron at Mount Magnet?' asked Mr Gibson.

'I did, and I also asked him if he could tell me of anyone who had seen him with Carron at any time after 18 May 1930,' said the police officer. 'He replied that he was not going to answer any questions, as he had told all he knew about Carron.'

Asked about the allegation that the Crown had withheld certain documents belonging to the accused, Manning denied that there was any truth in it. 'All the documents the police took from Rowles have been produced,' he said.

The last witness of all was Mrs Jay, the Youanmi postmistress, who gave evidence of having received from Rowles a letter addressed to Lemon, which the prisoner said explained all that he knew of Carron's whereabouts. The letter had been read in court during the course of Lemon's own evidence.

23. Carron alive in Canada?

Mr Curran made his address to the jury on the afternoon of the seventh day, claiming that the Crown had failed to establish that the remains found at the rabbit reserve were Carron's and that the facts which had been adduced were not inconsistent with his client's innocence.

'Because a man has disappeared in the Murchison district, it does not mean that he has been murdered, or even that he is dead,' he pointed out. 'Men go out into the heart of Australia prospecting very often, and, because they disappear, no one can say they are dead. They may come back.'

He described as absurd the Crown's contention that a man would commit a murder – 'and take so much trouble over it' – for the sake of a £25 cheque and a few paltry belongings, and went on to suggest that the objects found among the camp-fire ashes had not been identified at all satisfactorily.

Mrs Brown was the only one who had definitely identified the ring, he said – disregarding the evidence of Long the jeweller – and her grounds for doing so were weak. She could only say that it was her ring by a few marks on it, and many rings had the same marks. A dentist had said that a tooth was similar to one which he had filled for Carron, but only one tooth had been found and Carron had had several filled, Mr Curran continued. And who could say that the pieces of human skull came from Carron's remains? One doctor had even said that it was impossible to say whether the pieces came from an aboriginal's skull or a European's.

'The Crown witnesses will not assume the responsibility of identifying those remains,' declared Mr Curran. 'Why should you, gentlemen of the jury?'

He then asked the jury to consider the possibility that Carron, whom he said was a strange man in many ways, had left the country. Carron, who had sometimes told his wife that he was a Canadian, and at other times that he was a New Zealander, had left New Zealand under an assumed name, travelling as a single man. It was obvious, said Mr Curran, that he was trying to obscure his identity.

In support of this idea, he read the jury a long letter which Carron had written to his sister in New Zealand, beginning, 'So you see I am in Australia instead of Canada.' The letter told how Carron had had all his money stolen on the voyage to Fremantle, of his meeting with John Lemon in Perth, and of their journey to the Murchison together. It told of beer which he had drunk, of an attempt to get on a wheat ship at Geraldton, and of his dislike of Western Australia and its loneliness. The letter made it appear obvious that Carron had wanted to get to Canada, and the Perth police had been remiss in not advertising for him there, said Mr Curran.

Even if the remains found at the rabbit reserve *were* Carron's, the Crown had still not established that Rowles murdered him, the defence counsel continued. The Crown case, in a nutshell, was that Rowles and Carron left Lemon at the Narndee outcamp on 18 May, and that Rowles killed Carron, burnt his body, and appeared with his cheque in Paynesville on 20 May. But the occasion on which Julian O'Dea saw Rowles and Carron together in Mount Magnet could only have been *after* the date of the alleged murder, argued Mr Curran. So the case against the prisoner fell to the ground.

Mr Curran then dealt with Rowles's statement to Detective Sergeant Manning, saying that it contained just those minor discrepancies that one would expect to find in an unprepared statement made nearly a year after the events it described. He also dealt at length with the evidence which the prisoner had given the previous day, claiming that Rowles had given a very reasonable explanation of how Carron's belongings had been found in his possession.

Finally, after speaking for two hours, Mr Curran concluded his address by asking the jury to consider the evidence carefully and give Rowles the benefit of the reasonable doubt which he said must exist in their own minds about his client's guilt.

As it was then 5 p.m., the court adjourned to the following day.

24. An ideal place for such a crime

The eighth day was a Saturday: the first Saturday on which the Criminal Court had sat since 1924. The Crown Prosecutor began his address when the court opened, setting out the Crown's case for a verdict of guilty against the accused and making a vigorous attack on Rowles's defence. It was delivered in even, measured tones and lasted for three hours.

'Like most murder cases, this case is made up entirely of circumstantial evidence, except for some statements made by the accused,' Mr Gibson told the jury. 'You can put your own value on these statements. In considering the probabilities of the case, you must take the whole collection of facts presented to you.

'You have seen that throughout this trial Rowles has shown himself to be a shrewd, calm and collected man. At the time we say the crime was committed, Rowles had escaped from jail. You must remember that you are dealing with a type of crime that could be committed only by a man who was a shrewd, calm and thinking being.

'Counsel for the defence has brought out in his cross-examination that when Mr Moses saw Rowles on 20 May, at Paynesville, he showed no signs of being a man who had just committed a terrible crime. You have seen Rowles, gentlemen. I ask you, would he be likely to show any signs of agitation? He is quite cold.'

Dealing with the question of motive, Mr Gibson said that very often in murder cases it was impossible to show any motive, and that the onus was not on the Crown to supply one. In the present case, there was the motive of personal gain, of which they had direct evidence, and perhaps there was another motive of which they were unaware. He suggested that Rowles may have felt an enmity towards Carron which he did not display in the presence of other people.

Mr Gibson then told the story set out in the Crown case from the time of Carron's departure from New Zealand. He dealt with Carron's visit to Sims the dentist, the wedding ring which he wore on his little finger, and the two watches that he sent to Perth for repair, then went on to describe the circumstances which surrounded his disappearance.

168

He asked the jury to bear in mind that Rowles had already decided on a prospecting trip to Wiluna by the time he and Carron left Lemon's outcamp, as this showed that the reason he gave for being in Youanmi three days later was a fabrication.

'Is it feasible that Rowles would go on a long journey north to Windimurra Station and then return to Youanmi to get his tools when, if he had wanted them, he could have gone direct to Youanmi from Lemon's camp, a very much shorter journey?' argued Mr Gibson.

He claimed that the explanation had only been invented when the defence realized that it would be impossible to refute the evidence of Rowles's appearance in Youanmi on 21 May 1930.

Continuing his address, the Crown Prosecutor dealt with the discrepancies between Rowles's statement to Manning and the evidence which he had given in court, discrepancies which Mr Gibson regarded as far more important than Mr Curran was willing to concede.

Rowles had at first claimed that he and Carron camped at the old Windimurra homestead, but changed his statement after the owner and overseer of Windimurra both gave evidence to the effect that that was untrue. He had changed his story in respect of the number of days which he spent hunting with Carron before going into Paynesville. And, having originally said nothing about going into Youanmi, he had invented the story about going to get his prospecting tools after two witnesses testified that they had seen him there on 21 May.

'Mr Moses, the licensee of the Paynesville Hotel, says that Rowles left Paynesville that date at 10 a.m.,' said Mr Gibson. 'In his statement, Rowles said that on arriving back at Windimurra he had to wait two hours for Carron to come in to lunch, and yet there is ample evidence that Rowles arrived at Youanmi two and a half hours after leaving Paynesville, sixty-three miles away. Rowles's story of his coming back to Windimurra to his pal Carron is obviously a fabrication.'

The number of bottles of Globe beer which Rowles drank or gave away in Youanmi showed that his claim to have bought them to take back to Carron at the fox traps was just a blind, argued Mr Gibson. His story about Moses's cheque for £17 being in Carron's possession until Rowles cashed it for him on 22 May was untrue, as an entry in Jones's bar book showed that the Youanmi hotel proprietor had received it from Rowles on 21 May. Rowles was also known to have lied when he told Jones that Moses had given him the cheque in payment for some fox scalps.

Rowles had questioned Jones's book entries showing that he had booked in at the hotel on 21 May and stayed there continuously until 2 June, Mr Gibson continued. He claimed that he went back to Windimurra and rejoined Carron on the evening of 21 May, stayed the night with him there, hunted with him the following day, then went into Mount Magnet with him on the evening of 22 May, when they parted company.

'If he was not at the Youanmi Hotel, do you think he would have paid for his board and lodging for the period?' asked Mr Gibson.

There was also an entry on a docket, dated 22 May, showing that Rowles had purchased a pair of overalls at the hotel store that day, he pointed out.

'The whole story of his being at Windimurra Station with Carron and of his coming into Mount Magnet with him is a sheer concoction,' the Crown Prosecutor contended. 'The evidence of Lord, the manager of Windimurra, and Wilkins, his overseer, proves that Carron and Rowles were never at Windimurra, and there is ample evidence to show that Rowles was at Youanmi at that time.'

Moving on to the evidence of Julian O'Dea and Robert Broadbent, Mr Gibson accused both of these

170

witnesses of lying. Speaking of O'Dea's claim to have found Rowles and Carron having supper together at Mrs Slavin's shop after 20 May 1930, he said:

'If O'Dea was honest, do you think he would have said nothing of this alleged meeting with Carron to the police, who were searching for Carron? O'Dea is a man who has the audacity to say that he would let the accused go to his trial and say nothing about what he knew. He is a type who would let a man go to the gallows and say nothing. No doubt you will dismiss O'Dea from your mind as being not only an unreliable witness, but a dishonest one!'

Dealing with Broadbent's evidence, Mr Gibson said: 'Broadbent is an obvious liar. You saw him for yourself. His tale that Lemon and Carron were together on 21 January 1931, the very day that Lemon reported Carron's disappearance to the police, is ridiculous. He said that Lemon told him that tale in Perth, on a date when Lemon was over 500 miles away at Cue. Broadbent is another bright citizen like O'Dea!'

After pointing out to the jury on a plan that the area near the 183-mile gate, where the murder was allegedly committed, lay on the route Rowles and Carron would have taken from Narndee Station to Wiluna, Mr Gibson said that the spot would be an ideal one for committing such a crime.

'The old hut on the reserve had everything wrong with it,' he explained. 'It was old, and the timber was ant-eaten and rotten. The spot was secluded, and was visited only a few times a year by Maddison, the man who was patrolling the fence. It had only been visited, as far as Maddison knew, once in the past four years by passers-by.

'The defence claimed that a more likely place would have been selected by Rowles if he had contemplated such a crime, but witnesses have told you that any tracks seen cutting through the bush at random were likely to

171

be followed, and any fires out in open country investigated. It was not so with tracks leading to a hut or bore, nor with fires in such localities.

'It was also an ideal spot for disposing of human remains by burning them, as good timber is to be had in the vicinity.'

Later in his address, Mr Gibson directed the jury's attention to the fact that Rowles had asked for twenty gallons of petrol at Paynesville and had been supplied with sixteen gallons. He told Moses that he wanted this petrol for a trip to Wiluna, but 'might have wanted it for a different purpose altogether', said Mr Gibson.

The Crown Prosecutor then reviewed the evidence concerning the discoveries made at the rabbit reserve, which he said showed that the remains were definitely Carron's.

He said Carron had possessed a gold faceted wedding ring, with certain peculiar markings; he had a complete lower set of diatoric teeth; he had had an upper molar filled on the biting surface; he carried a cardboard box made with metal stitches of a type that were identifiable, and he wore sandshoes.

Such a ring, with the same markings; similar teeth; eyelets that might reasonably have come from sandshoes, and ten metal stitches – the same number as in Carron's box – were all found in the ashes on the rabbit reserve, Mr Gibson continued.

'I don't think that you gentlemen can come to any other conclusion than that Carron's body was burnt in those fires,' he argued, adding: 'Having reached that conclusion, I don't think you will have much difficulty in deciding who killed Carron.'

He then dealt with Rowles's account of how Carron's belongings had come into his possession, holding his explanations up to ridicule.

25. Rowles sentenced to death

When the Crown Prosecutor concluded his address at 2.30 p.m., Mr Justice Draper began his summing-up. He told the jury that they must find the prisoner either guilty or not guilty of wilful murder, as there was no other alternative before them.

'You have been told that the evidence in this case is purely circumstantial,' he said. 'You must realize that in all murder cases circumstantial evidence preponderates. It is natural that all crimes are committed as secretly as possible, especially wilful murder. Circumstantial evidence is evidence from which inferences of guilt or innocence may be drawn. It consists not only of actual events proved, but of matters relating to the behaviour of the accused, including his making of statements. It is important to ascertain what, if anything, an accused person is concealing in his statements. An accused may make statements which impute guilt to himself.

'In this case, Rowles has made statements which are hard to reconcile with his being innocent of some crime, and the question to be decided is, what crime? You have the story of his movements, and you have his statements. You have to consider all the evidence, and you may find it difficult to reconcile his statements with the evidence. There are minor discrepancies in his statements which might be explained by the length of time that had elapsed between the incidents described and the taking of the statements. You must, however, look at the material discrepancies, which cannot be explained by the lapse of time.'

The judge dealt briefly with the question of motive, saying that if the Crown case was correct, Rowles had got Carron's cheque and all his property. Carron had been murdered and certain of his belongings, and part of his remains, were found in the ashes on the rabbit reserve, he continued. The bones had been broken up

173

into little pieces, and distributed among heaps of ashes which had apparently been taken from a main fire when they were cold.

'There is a curious thing in this case, which may be mentioned for what it is worth,' said the judge. 'Upfield, who is a budding author, gave evidence that he was in the neighbourhood for some time. He says he remembers a discussion one night in a small room, when the accused, among others, was present, in October 1929. The interesting subject of discussion was how a human body could be destroyed without leaving a trace. It was proposed by Mr George Ritchie that the best way would be to burn the body, and crush the bones remaining after the ashes of the fire were cold. The bones found in the ashes I have referred to were certainly crushed up.'

On the question of whether Carron might still be alive, Mr Justice Draper said that he had certainly never been seen since the police began looking for him, and that his goods were found in Rowles's possession. O'Dea's evidence was too vague and unsatisfactory for much notice to be taken of it, and this witness had not thought it necessary to inform the police of the important evidence which he claimed he could give. So, in deciding whether Carron was alive or dead – the first important task confronting them – the judge said that the jury would have to be guided principally by the human remains which had been found.

He went on to say that the ring found among the ashes had been definitely identified by Carron's wife and by the jeweller who sold it to her. 'If the ring is not enough to satisfy you that the remains in the ashes were Carron's, what if other belongings of Carron's were found in the ashes?' he asked. 'It would indeed be a strange coincidence. We have the teeth, and it is for you to decide if they are Carron's. If you come to the conclusion that they are, you must ask yourselves how they got there, and you must remember the pieces of skull. If you are satisfied that Carron was murdered, you have then to decide by whom.'

The judge then dealt with the prisoner's account of how Carron's goods came to be found in his possession. He said that it was obvious that Rowles knew about the petrol case containing Carron's overcoat, as some of his own documents were found inside it. His suggestion that Carron must have substituted his Omega watch for the one in the dashboard of Rowles's truck might have been all right if it were the only thing to be explained, but there was also Carron's wristwatch found in a parcel in Rowles's camp. Having been repaired by Levinson and Sons for Carron, this was known to have been sent for repair a second time by Rowles after Carron's alleged murder.

Mr Justice Draper went on to deal with other articles found in Rowles's possession, then turned to the question of his alleged suicide attempts. He said that Rowles may have preferred suicide as the easiest way out after his arrest, but his claim to have swallowed strychine was a different story from his attempted hanging, and was probably a product of his excited imagination.

In concluding, the judge told the jury that they must be convinced that the facts brought out in evidence were not only consistent with the accused being guilty, but inconsistent with any other conclusion. If they were satisfied that there was no other rational conclusion to be drawn from the evidence, then they must bring in a verdict accordingly, he said.

*

Having retired at five minutes to four that afternoon, the jury returned to give their verdict at six o'clock. As they entered, all eyes in the courtroom turned towards them, and most realized from their grim appearance what verdict they had reached.

The prisoner stood on the steps leading from the dock to the cells below, waiting for the judge to take his seat. He could not see the faces of the jurymen from there, even when he craned his neck, and so turned to look at the massed witnesses.

The judge then returned to his seat and the prisoner took his place in the dock. He stared at the jury and was seen to shake his head, as if he, too, now knew that he was doomed.

On being asked what verdict the jury had reached, the foreman replied in a husky voice, 'Guilty!'

A deathly silence followed, lasting a few seconds, then Rowles was asked whether he had anything to say before sentence was passed. In a clear, steady voice, he replied, 'I have been found guilty of a crime that has never been committed.'

'Is that all?' asked the judge. 'Is that all you have to say?'

The prisoner declined to answer, and the court remained silent until the judge began pronouncing sentence of death.

26. A plea which he ignored

To many people, the result was a foregone conclusion. Public opinion had been strongly against Rowles before the trial started, as a result of the revelations made at the inquest, and the evidence produced in his defence could hardly have helped to raise doubts about his guilt. It was, nonetheless, a sensational trial, with many dramatic developments, and a newspaper report two days later described it as 'one of the most remarkable in the criminal annals of Western Australia'.

Rowles appealed to the State Supreme Court, claiming that some of the evidence given against him – including that which concerned the disappearance of James Ryan and George Lloyd – had been wrongfully admitted. He also claimed that the judge had misdirected the jury, that there was no evidence that Carron was dead, and that the trial had resulted in a miscarriage of justice. But when the appeal was heard by the Full Court of Western Australia it was unanimously dismissed.

The condemned man then applied for leave to appeal to the High Court of Australia, and this court, sitting in Melbourne, devoted a whole day to hearing the application on 26 May. The proceedings on this occasion were marked by spirited exchanges between Mr Justice Starke, one of the five judges, and Dr Brennan, KC, who appeared for Rowles, on the desirability of listing such cases for appeal to the High Court. The hearing ended with a majority decision to reject the application.

When Western Australia's Executive Council considered the question of Rowles's fate on 31 May, it decided against commuting his sentence. His death warrant was then signed and his execution fixed for Monday, 13 June – which allowed for two clear Sundays to elapse after confirmation of the sentence, as the law required.

Rowles was not without sympathizers among the public. The Attorney General, Mr T.A.L. Davy, received a deputation representing the Groper Brotherhood, the Housewives' Association and the Hotel and Restaurant Employees' Union, and promised to place their request for a reconsideration of his sentence before the Government. There were also letters written to newspapers, appealing for clemency to be shown, for the sake of the prisoner's mother.

A few days after the death warrant was signed, Rowles made a statement from his condemned cell in Fremantle Prison, in which he finally admitted that the remains found at the rabbit reserve were Carron's, but again denied murdering him.

He said that on returning from Paynesville, he found that Carron had accidentally poisoned himself with butter-baits which had been intended for the foxes, and that his body had been attacked by crows. Rowles's first impulse, according to this new account, was to report the matter to the police, but being an escaped prisoner, he feared that he would not be believed. He therefore decided to dispose of the body and say nothing about it.

The statement was handed to the Attorney General by Rowles's counsel, Mr F. Curran, on 6 June. Mr Curran said that he had first obtained it verbally two days earlier, when he went to see Rowles for the purpose of drawing up his will. He then arranged for it to be taken down for Rowles to sign.

The statement, together with a petition presented by the Groper Brotherhood and the Housewives' Association, was placed before the Executive Council the following day, but again no commutation was granted. The law was to be left to take its course.

Four days before it did so, George Lloyd's brother Charles, living in Adelaide, sent a telegram to the Sheriff of the Supreme Court of Western Australia. It read: 'Ask Rowles before his execution whether he will enlighten our family about my brother George's supposed death, which would end the dreadful suspense for our mother, who is in delicate health.'

Lloyd revealed that some teeth which Detective Sergeant Manning had sent him for examination resembled those of his missing brother, but that he could not identify them with certainty. His mother, he said, still clung to the hope that George was still alive.

Rowles made no attempt to alleviate Mrs Lloyd's suffering. On the Saturday before he was hanged, he gave Mr Curran a letter in which he again protested his innocence of Carron's murder and denied knowing the fate of the other two men. He made no further statement on either subject.

On the morning of his execution, 13 June 1932, he maintained the air of fortitude which he had displayed at his trial, walking firmly towards the scaffold. The official announcement that the sentence had been carried out gave his name as John Thomas Smith only.

*

So ended this unusual case, in which a mystery writer's search for an original plot led to murder in real life. There can be little doubt that Rowles had killed Ryan and Lloyd as well as Carron, and disposed of their bodies at Challi Bore. It is also clear that all three murders were committed in cold blood, for the sake of personal gain.

Rowles, like so many other callous murderers, was a known criminal. In 1926, he had snatched a bag containing £300 from a shopgirl in Perth; two years later, he had robbed a number of country stores on the eastern wheat-belt. The murders of Ryan, Lloyd and Carron all took place after he had escaped from Dalwallinu, following his conviction for burglary.

But he was also – like Richard Brinkley – astonishingly careless. He murdered his victims after being seen in their company, failed to destroy their bodies thoroughly enough to avoid detection and kept objects of little value which linked him to the crimes. He even took gratuitous risks by telling lies which were inconsistent with each other.

So, although on some occasions he did indeed behave like a 'shrewd, calm and collected man' – as the prosecutor at his trial called him – he did not do so consistently. Sometimes he did just the opposite, as if unconsciously trying to draw suspicion upon himself. It was only after he had been arrested, and realized that he was in a desperate situation, that he really began to merit Mr Gibson's description.

By that time, he had little chance of saving himself.

SURVIVORS OF THE DEATH PENALTY

The Cases of John Smith, Margaret Dickson, James Buchanan, Joseph Samuel, John Lee, Will Purvis and Willie Francis

1. Hanged – then pardoned

A convicted housebreaker named John Smith was a well-known figure in London during the first three decades of the eighteenth century. He had the unenviable distinction of having once been hanged at Tyburn – only to be cut down and resuscitated on the late arrival of a reprieve. A notorious offender, he was commonly called 'Half-Hanged' Smith, in consequence of this bizarre experience.

Smith was a native of Malton, near York, where he was born about 1662. The son of a farmer, he was sent to London in his youth to serve an apprenticeship with a packer, and continued in that trade as a journeyman for some time before deciding to go to sea. He then served first aboard a merchant ship and afterwards on a man-of-war, in which he is known to have taken part in the attack on Vigo Bay on 12 October 1702. He later claimed that in that battle, in which a Spanish fleet was destroyed, he was wounded in both hands.

On returning to London, he was discharged from the naval service and enlisted in the Second Regiment of Foot Guards, commanded by Lord Cutts. Soon, like many of his fellow soldiers, he was regularly involved in housebreaking and theft, a course on which he seems to have started some years earlier – perhaps even before going to sea – if the evidence of an accomplice is to be believed. On 5 December 1705, he was arraigned at the Old Bailey on four separate indictments, having been apprehended two days earlier.

The crimes with which he was charged, according to

an account published in 1718, were: (1) breaking into a shop near Leadenhall Market and stealing fifty pairs of men's shoes (date not given); (2) breaking into a warehouse in Mincing Lane and stealing 900 yards of cloth on 5 November the same year; (3) breaking into a warehouse (location not given) and stealing 400 lb of China silk, value £350, on 28 February the same year; and (4) breaking into a shop (location not given) and stealing 148 pairs of gloves and twenty-two pairs of stockings on 3 December the same year. All were capital offences, as were a great many crimes at this time.

In the first case it was alleged that the offence had been committed by Smith and an accomplice, the two men breaking open the shop door and stealing the goods at about six o'clock in the morning. Smith denied the charge, but the accomplice gave evidence against him, confessing that he and the prisoner had been thieving together for six or seven years. Smith was found guilty.

In the second, in which it was claimed that Smith and two others had committed the robbery and shared the goods between them, the evidence also appears to have been quite strong, for one of the alleged accomplices and the wife of the other both appeared against him. It seems, however, that he was not convicted in this case, though the 1718 account – the earliest detailed one which has come to light – does not tell us the outcome of it.

On the charge of stealing the China silk he was acquitted for lack of evidence. But on the one which concerned the crime of 3 December – when he was caught red-handed on the premises, with the gloves and stockings bundled up in readiness to be carried off – he was found guilty.

After being sentenced to death, John Smith was put into the Condemned Hold of Newgate Prison, a dark and insanitary place where those awaiting execution spent their last days. He was not resigned to his fate, for many capital offenders were reprieved and he had been given cause to hope that he might be one of them. However, no reprieve came for him, and on 12 December the hanging cart came instead.

He was, as far as we know, the only person due to be hanged on this occasion, and he was not yet well known. But as hanging days were public holidays, it is likely that there were many people waiting to watch the awe-inspiring procession to the gallows.

Before he left the prison the condemned man's irons were struck off and his arms bound from behind with rope; another rope – the one with which he was to be hanged – was tied loosely round his neck or chest. The Ordinary of Newgate (the prison chaplain) rode with him in the open cart, to exhort him to repentance.

The gallows at Tyburn was a large triangular structure with three overhead beams, known as the Triple Tree. Each of the beams was large enough for eight people to be hanged from it without touching each other, and multiple executions were frequently carried out there. The condemned were hanged from the tail of the cart.

Smith had at first been bitter about being denied a reprieve, but at the place of execution expressed the hope that all present would take warning from his untimely death, which he said none but himself by his sins had brought him to. He was turned off after performing 'the usual devotions', the hangman pulling his legs in order to prevent him suffering unnecessarily.

But after he had been hanging for some time – about seven minutes by one account, fifteen by others – and appeared to be dead, a horseman arrived with the news that he had been reprieved after all. He was therefore cut down from the gallows and hastily conveyed to a nearby public house, where, according to Narcissus Luttrell (a diarist of the time), he was 'immediately lett blood and put into a warm bed, which, with other applications, brought him to himself again with much adoe'. Later the same day he was taken back to Newgate.

Having already excited the admiration of those who had come to see him hanged, he became the centre of attention in the prison, and no doubt many people paid to be allowed in to see him, as often happened when a famous criminal was confined there. The 1718 account tells us that he described his experience by saying that after being turned off

> he for some time was sensible of a very great Pain, occasioned by the Weight of his Body, and felt his Spirits in a strange Commotion, violently pressing upwards ... to his Head, [when] he as it were saw a great Blaze or glaring Light, which seemed to go out at his Eyes as it were with a Flash, and then he lost all sense of Pain.

When he began to revive, he continued, 'the Blood and Spirits ... forcing themselves into their former Channels ... put him by a sort of pricking or shooting to so intolerable a Pain ... that he could have wish'd those hang'd that had cut him down'.

A reprieve in those days was not a commutation of sentence; it was merely a postponement of execution, generally for a week or a fortnight while the desirability of a commutation – i.e., a conditional pardon – or a free pardon was being considered.

Pardons, whether free or conditional, were generally granted in batches, the prisoners whose cases had been received with favour being first given leave to plead 'at the next general pardon' in the courts in which they had been sentenced. In a report of the proceedings at the Old Bailey published in one newspaper – *The Post Boy* of 31 August to 3 September 1700 – we find the following description of this procedure:

The last Day of the Sessions 85 Criminals Pleaded on

their Knees the Kings most Gracious Pardon, acknowledging his Majesties great Clemency and Mercy; they presented the Court with Gloves according to Custom; most of them are to be Transported to our American Plantations, and not to return to this Kingdom within the space of 7 Years, on pain of Death.

In Smith's case the reprieve was followed by an unconditional pardon, which he pleaded on 20 February 1706, and was thereupon released. It may well have been granted to him in return for disclosures about other offenders, for we know from Luttrell's diary that by 3 March he had accused about 350 'pick-pockets, house breakers, &c., who gott to be soldiers in the guards, the better to hide their roguery', and that on that day, when the regiments were mustered, these were all drawn out to be shipped off to Spain, together with about sixty women who lay under condemnation for similar offences.

The following November, Smith and two other men denounced another two sergeants and six soldiers of the Second Regiment as 'felons and housebreakers'. But after being committed to prison, these were all discharged for lack of evidence.

How Smith made his living after being released from Newgate is not known, but at some stage during the next nine years he kept a public house in Southwark. At any rate, he managed to avoid getting into any further trouble with the law for the whole of that period. But eventually his dissolute ways led him back into crime – if he had ever really given it up – and on the morning of 28 January 1715 he was apprehended in Rood Lane, a turning off Fenchurch Street, after breaking into a nearby warehouse.

He was indicted at the Old Bailey at the February Sessions, and appeared for trial two months later. It was then revealed that the premises in question – which was

187

part of a dwelling-house – had been broken into on three previous occasions and goods stolen each time. Because of this, the warehouseman had left two watchmen to guard it overnight.

About five o'clock in the morning, the door was broken open and the prisoner entered, unaware that anyone else was there. One of the watchmen struck at him but missed, and Smith then fled from the building with both of them in pursuit. When he was caught and searched at the end of Rood Lane, the padlock which had been wrenched from the door was found in his possession, together with several picklock keys and a tobacco box with tinder and matches in it.

The indictment on which he was tried charged him with burglary, but of the warehouseman's premises rather than the householder's. This mistake was no doubt caused by the warehouseman's eagerness to see justice done, for in those days the victim of the crime was usually the prosecutor. But the result was confusion.

The jury accepted that the facts alleged against the prisoner were proved, but could not decide whether they amounted to burglary, or, if so, of which premises. They therefore brought in a special verdict, referring the case to a panel of judges, and Smith was committed to Newgate to await the outcome. He remained there for eighteen months.

Finally, on 10 November 1716, the decision of the judges was announced – and this, as may be expected, was in his favour. By this time, a second indictment, charging him in the name of the householder, could not be proceeded with, as the householder, being now dead, could not prosecute him. Smith, who was by now very well known, had therefore to be released.

The 1718 account concludes by stating that he then 'began to play his old Game again, for which he is now a Prisoner in the Work-house, where for the present we shall leave him'. To find out what happened to him after that, we have to turn to the newspapers and printed *Old Bailey Sessions Papers* of the time, for later accounts do not tell us. From these contemporary sources, however, we learn of further crimes of which he was accused.

On 7 May 1720, about three o'clock in the morning, a passer-by named Robert Nicholson saw Smith leaving a cellar in Mincing Lane. Finding that the door had been broken open and the padlock taken, he roused the owner's servant, and between them they apprehended the suspect in the street.

Although the padlock was not found in his possession, and he denied all knowledge of the affair, Smith was again committed for trial. Reporting this on 14 May, *The Weekly Journal or Saturday's-Post* reminded its readers that the prisoner had once been hanged at Tyburn. It went on to comment, '[How] it may go with him this Time, we cannot pretend to say; but it looks as if he was not born to be drowned.'

Charged with stealing the padlock, Smith appeared for trial at the Old Bailey Sessions of 2–3 June. The *Sessions Papers* give his name as John Smith, alias Wilson, and tell us:

> Robert Nicholson deposed that as he was going to work about 3 a Clock in the Morning the Day aforesaid, he saw the Prisoner and another Man on St. Dunstan's-Hill, who parted, that he follow'd the other Man, who had a Bag on his Shoulder, and the Prisoner went the other Way; that this Evidence went to the Tackle House, and coming back to Mincing Lane saw Mr. Grew's Vault Door pusht open, and the Prisoner come out of it.

The owner's servant confirmed that the padlock had been missing when Nicholson woke him up at three o'clock, and said that when Smith was asked for it he told them that the man who had been with him earlier had it. However, the man who had once been hanged had a different story to tell:

> The Prisoner denied the Fact, and said that he has a Wife in St. Thomas's Hospital, and a Child at Nurse in Southwark, and that going along they seized him, and ask'd him for the Lock, and what was become of the Man that was with him; to which he reply'd he had no Body with him, nor knew nothing of the Lock; and that if they had lost one, the Man whom they talkt of might have it.

The jury acquitted him.

A year and a half later, during the early morning of 12 September 1721, Smith was seen emerging from a warehouse, also in Mincing Lane. He was arrested and searched, and eight picklock keys and a tinder-box were found – but again he had no stolen property. This time he was charged only with a misdemeanour, for which he was tried at the Old Bailey Sessions of 11–14 October.

The *Sessions Papers* record that 'John Smith, (commonly called Half-Hang'd Smith)' denied the offence and called witnesses to his character, but 'the Fact being fully proved, and he being known to be a Notorious Offender, the Jury found him Guilty'. The summary concludes: 'Fined 40 Marks (£26 13s 4d), to suffer 3 Years Imprisonment, and to find security for his good behaviour for 3 Years after.'

Though the case was a minor one, a number of paragraphs were published in connection with it, showing that he was still a well-known figure. But when he made his final appearance in the same court five and a half years later his name was merely recorded as John Wilson, alias Smith, and he was apparently not recognized as an old offender.

The case on that occasion was similar in some respects to that of 1720. Smith and an accomplice were apprehended by two watchmen after attempting to break into a warehouse, but the second man managed to escape. Smith was not so lucky, and, having the padlock from the warehouse door in his possession, tried to dispose of it before it was discovered. He was not successful, and was charged with stealing it.

The padlock was produced at his trial, together with eight picklock keys found in his pocket. The *Sessions Papers* state that 'it appearing by several plain Circumstances that he took the Padlock with a design to rob the Warehouse, the Jury found him guilty of single Felony'. He was sentenced to be transported to Virginia, as North America was then called.

It was now twenty-two years since he had been hanged, and his luck had run out completely. No specific term of transportation is recorded in his case, but the sentence was undoubtedly one of seven or fourteen years. So if he survived the outward journey – and many convicts did not – there was little chance of his living long enough to complete his term among the plantations.

In a petition praying for a mitigation of sentence, addressed to the Lord Mayor of London, Smith declared that he was in his sixty-sixth year, with 'much decay'd' sight, and that he had a poor wife and two children. He had been wounded in both hands at Vigo, and had afterwards served as a soldier in Lord Cutts's Regiment, he pointed out. But this was to no avail, and towards the end of the following month he was one of a party of felons taken from Newgate to begin the journey to America.

He had evaded justice, such as it was, for the last time.

2. A noise from inside the coffin

Margaret Dickson, a young married Scotswoman, became well known for the same reason as John Smith, though she had little else in common with him. A native of Musselburgh, a small town six miles to the east of Edinburgh, she was separated from her husband, and early in 1723 arrived at Maxwell Heugh, in the parish of Kelso, about thirty-seven miles south-east of her home town. She remained there for the rest of the year.

On 9 December, the body of a newborn child was found in the River Tweed, not far from where she was staying, and a search was made for any woman in the district who had recently given birth in secret. Margaret was found to have done so, and confessed that the dead child was hers. She said it had been born dead and that she had kept its body hidden in her bed for seven or eight days. She had then taken it down to the river and left it there on the morning of its discovery.

As she had concealed her pregnancy and not called for help at the time of giving birth, it was not believed that the child had been stillborn, and Margaret was accused of its murder. She was committed to prison to await trial, and several months later – in July 1724 – appeared before the High Court of Justiciary in Edinburgh.

The case against her was a tenuous one. Four witnesses told the court of her confession – which she had since retracted – including a country midwife and two other women who had taken part in the search for the dead child's mother. It was also claimed that the child had gone its full time in the womb; that it had nails and hair, and that the prisoner had had 'green milk in her breast and several other signs of a woman lately brought to bed'.

But there was no real evidence that the child had been murdered, and in place of such evidence it could only be asserted that 'a woman that was so unnatural as to throw her child into the river in such a clandestine way, early in the morning, will easily be presumed to have murdered him'.

In her defence it was pointed out that the prisoner's husband was still living in Musselburgh, which was near enough to Kelso for him to have been with her frequently during the nine or ten months since she had left him. She could therefore not be presumed to have had such a strong motive for murdering the child as an unmarried woman, who might have been tempted from fear of shame.

Despite the slenderness of the case against her, the jury returned a verdict of guilty, and Margaret Dickson was sentenced to death. No doubt the sentence was pronounced in the usual way by John Dalgleish, the Edinburgh hangman, for he, as dempster (or doomster) to the court, had the duty of pronouncing all such sentences. Four more weeks then elapsed before she was taken out to be hanged; four weeks in which she lay in the Edinburgh Tolbooth, reflecting on the events which had led to her condemnation.

Towards the end – for she had no inkling that it would *not* be the end – a four-page pamphlet, described as her *Last Speech, Confession and Warning,* was prepared for publication after her death. This gives an account of the case from her own point of view, and contains many details not recorded elsewhere.

From it we learn that Margaret was the daughter of a god-fearing Protestant couple, and that she had been married, at the age of about nineteen, against her parents' wishes. Her husband failed to provide for her after the birth of their first child, and went off and left her when she became pregnant again. She had therefore to fend for herself as best she could, and did so for the next three years.

Early in 1723, she left her two children in Musselburgh and set out to visit two aunts who lived in Newcastle. But on reaching the village of Maxwell Heugh, she was offered work at the home of a family named Bell, and decided to stay there for a while instead.

It was there that the tragedy leading to her condemnation occurred.

Margaret accused William Bell, one of her employer's sons, of being the man responsible for her third pregnancy. She claimed that the occasion on which the child was conceived was the only time that she had ever been intimate with any man except her husband, and that the act had only taken place because Bell got drunk one night and forced himself upon her while she was asleep.

Although she told him of her condition, she kept it hidden from the other members of the family, and was even able to give birth in secret while pretending that she was suffering from colic. It was William Bell's brother who discovered the child's body and raised the alarm the day she put it into the river.

While still denying that she had murdered the child, Margaret acknowledged the justness of her sentence. This was presumably because the child had been alive when she went into labour and she saw her failure to call for help as being the cause of its death. At any rate, she persisted in her denials to the end, even while regarding herself as 'a poor guilty criminal' and warning others to learn from her example, 'that they may not go astray as I have done'.

Sentenced on 3 August, she was hanged on the afternoon of 2 September, her execution being carried out according to custom in the Grassmarket, where a gibbet was erected on a massive block of sandstone known as the Gallows Stone. There were thousands of spectators present, and armed soldiers stood in attendance to prevent any attempt at a rescue. Being by this time imbued with religious fervour, Margaret undoubtedly prayed and confessed her sins in earnest before the hangman set about his work.

After being 'turned off', she was left hanging for about half an hour, and during the course of that time her legs were pulled by the hangman (as Smith's had been), so there was no cause for anyone to suspect that she was still alive. She was then cut down and nailed into a coffin by friends at the foot of the gibbet.

The friends placed the coffin on a cart, intending to take it to Musselburgh for burial in the Inveresk parish churchyard. But as they left the city, some surgeons' apprentices tried to steal the 'body' – the demand for subjects for dissection being at this time far greater than could be met by lawful means – and a scuffle resulted.

Margaret's friends managed to prevent her falling into the hands of these anatomists, and continued on their way. But the coffin had been damaged in the struggle and air had been let into it. This was afterwards seen as one of two reasons for her revival, the other being the jolting of the cart.

Reaching a village called Peppermill, the friends stopped for refreshment, leaving the cart unguarded in the road. While they were away, two joiners came out of a nearby house to view the coffin, out of curiosity, and were alarmed to hear a noise coming from inside it.

They informed Margaret's friends of this, demanding that the coffin be opened, and when this was done – with some reluctance – the hanged woman's limbs were seen to move. This naturally caused much excitement, and one of those present, a practitioner of phlebotomy (bloodletting) named Peter Purdie, opened one of her veins. She was then heard to groan, 'Oh, dear! Oh, dear!'

These signs of life encouraged the others to move her to a nearby hillside, where the blood returned to her lips and cheeks. Later, she was placed on blankets in a corn cart and taken the rest of the way to Musselburgh, with another woman attending her. She was still alive on arrival.

Kept in the town overnight on the orders of local magistrates, she was given restoratives and means of sustenance, and a minister prayed over her. The following morning she was taken to the home of her brother James, a weaver, and put into bed there.

'She had little Appearance of recovering her Health or Senses next Day, and cry'd out, to let her be gone, for she was to be executed on Wednesday,' a contemporary account informs us.

Her survival was nonetheless seen as miraculous, and people flocked from all around to see her, many of them giving her money before they left the house.

It was not long before her condition began to improve, and on 6 September – the Sunday after she was hanged – she was well enough to go to church. But her appearance caused such a sensation that the minister had to conduct her out of the churchyard, for fear that she would be trampled on by the crowds.

No attempt was made to apprehend her, for in such cases in Scotland it was considered that the sentence of the court had been carried out once the prisoner was cut down from the gallows. Margaret was therefore a free woman again, as well as an object of wonder.

Grateful for her deliverance, she spent the next Wednesday (9 September) in fasting and prayer, and said that she intended to do the same thing every week for the rest of her life.

Her unhappy marriage had, under Scottish law, been dissolved by her abortive execution. But the following month it was reported that she and her former husband had remarried. No doubt he was now one of her numerous admirers, and promised to treat her better than before. But whether he actually did so for any length of time we do not know.

This, in fact, is all that we are able to learn about 'Half-Hangit' Maggie Dickson from such contemporary publications and documents as have come to light. Later accounts tell us that she lived for many more years, and sold salt through the streets of Edinburgh, where she was a familiar figure. Unfortunately, the source of this information is unknown, so we cannot ascertain whether it is true.

Most accounts of this remarkable case are quite unreliable.

3. A rescue at Execution Dock

A third person to survive the death penalty during the eighteenth century was James Buchanan, a Scottish mariner hanged in 1738. In his case there was no late reprieve and no mistake: the condemned was cut down alive deliberately and carried off to safety by a party of his fellow sailors, after a struggle with officials attending the execution. This amazing rescue took place at Execution Dock, in Wapping, where Buchanan had been hanged in accordance with maritime custom.

Buchanan's crime had been committed on 16 October the previous year, aboard the *Royal Guardian*, an English merchant ship lying at anchor in the Canton River, in China. Buchanan, the ship's sail-maker, had been aboard another East Indiaman earlier in the day, and had brought two other Scotsmen back with him, to treat them to some punch. But while they were there a number of small boats arrived alongside the ship, and the *Royal Guardian's* fourth mate, a bad-tempered fellow named Michael Smith, drove him out onto the deck to begin stowing goods.

This led to a heated argument, and blows were struck in the darkness. Smith was stabbed three times, receiving wounds from which he died nineteen hours later.

The sail-maker denied the offence, but was not believed. Smith, on his deathbed, had accused him of the crime, and Buchanan, on an earlier occasion, had told others that he would kill Smith and that they would see him do it. Although the murder weapon had not been found in his possession, he could easily have thrown it overboard after the blows had been struck. He was therefore brought back to England in irons, and appeared for trial before the Court of Admiralty on 10 November 1738. On being convicted of murder, he was sentenced to death.

Buchanan, a thirty-one-year-old native of Stirlingshire, had gone to sea at the age of fifteen, and had worked on merchant vessels ever since. He was good-natured, hard-working and, unlike Michael Smith, well-liked. When his former shipmates heard that he was to be hanged, they saw him as the victim of a grave injustice.

For the next few weeks he lay in a condemned cell in Newgate Prison, one of fifteen such cells which had taken the place of the old Condemned Hold where John Smith was confined. He continued to maintain that he was innocent until he learnt that he had been denied a commutation of sentence. But then, in a state of consternation, he confessed his guilt, complaining of the fourth mate's severity and surliness, and claiming that he had only dealt the fatal blows after he himself had been struck for no reason.

Having unburdened his conscience thus, the former sail-maker of the *Royal Guardian* prepared himself for death at the hands of the common hangman.

It was customary in those days for capital offenders whose crimes had been committed at sea to be hanged at Execution Dock, on the bank of the Thames. The march from Newgate in such cases was headed by an official carrying a silver oar – the insignia of the Admiralty – on his shoulder, but the condemned rode in the back of a cart like those destined for Tyburn. The executions were carried out on a scaffold erected on the foreshore, the prisoners having to stand on a stage or platform, which would then be removed in order to leave them suspended.

On the morning that Buchanan was hanged, 20 December 1738, it was bitterly cold. A wind blew from the north-east, snow clung to the roofs of nearby warehouses, and ice formed at the river's edge. But the prisoner, having taken the sacrament before he left Newgate, maintained a devout attitude at the place of execution. According to an account of his behaviour written by the Ordinary, 'he appeared with abundance of Resolution, and was very serious at Prayers and singing of Psalms'. Repeating his confession, he said that his sentence was just.

He desired his Brother Sailors to beware of Passion, which was the Occasion of his being brought thither. He confessed that he was a great Sabbath-breaker, and observ'd that it was on the Lord's Day he murder'd Michael Smith; and also, that he had been a great Swearer and Drinker, and not free from other Vices.

He led the company on the scaffold in singing the twenty-third Psalm, and called on God to have mercy upon him. 'Lord Jesus receive my spirit,' he said as the stage was drawn from under him.

Buchanan having been hanged, the Ordinary took it for granted that he would be dead within a few minutes at the most, and so hurried off to prepare his account of the case for publication, one of the perquisites of his office. But almost immediately afterwards a number of seamen got onto the scaffold and tried to cut the offender down.

The officials resisted them, and a struggle took place, but then more seamen joined in and the attempt succeeded. Buchanan, still alive, was taken from the scaffold to a boat waiting nearby, and carried off towards Deptford with cries of jubilation.

At least sixty sailors were involved in the rescue, and it seems that after the initial struggle on the scaffold little was done to thwart them. A report written for the *Gentleman's Magazine* concluded:

The Compassion thus shewn this Criminal by his Brother Tars, is said to arise from his good Character, and being without Cause more severely beat by Smith who was a petty Officer, than any Englishman ought to bear without resenting.

To those in authority, however, it was a lawless act, an outrage perpetrated by 'evil-disposed' persons. Offers of rewards and pardons were accordingly made in an attempt to bring some of those concerned to justice, but apparently without success. A £200 reward for the apprehension of Buchanan himself was likewise made in vain.

What became of him is not known. Probably he took refuge abroad, rather than spend the rest of his life in hiding, but this is merely supposition. All we know for certain is that he was never recaptured.

4. Three times hanged – and still he lived

Joseph Samuel was an English Jew who became known in Australia in the early nineteenth century as 'the man they could not hang'. His story begins in London in May 1795, when, at the age of fourteen, he stood trial for his life at the Old Bailey. It seems that he was then a servant or an apprentice of some sort, for he claimed to have been at the home of his 'master' at the time of the alleged offence.

Samuel was charged in connection with a crime which had taken place in Moorfields during the early morning of 10 May, when a house in Chiswell Street was broken into and various household goods and articles of clothing stolen. He had not been apprehended at the scene of the crime, and none of the stolen property was found in his possession. But a servant from a house across the road claimed to have seen the culprits – two men and a boy –

at work from an upstairs window, and identified Samuel as the boy in question.

Though the prisoner claimed to have been elsewhere at the time, nobody was called to corroborate this, and he was convicted of simple larceny. This, however, was not a capital offence, and he was sentenced to seven years' transportation.

He spent the next six years in an English jail or prison hulk, awaiting a place on a convict ship to Australia – transportation to America having been brought to an end by the War of Independence – and finally left England on 21 June 1801. As the voyage to Sydney took almost six months, he arrived there with only a short time left to serve.

Probably, like most of the other convicts in this newly established colony, he was put to work on some Government construction project or assigned to a free settler in need of labour. Either way, he would have had a certain amount of freedom, but still been subject to the harsh discipline then in force. However, he had only to endure this for a few months before he became a free man himself, and it appears that he did so without getting into any further trouble. But the following year (1803) he committed the crime for which he was hanged.

Since his arrival in Sydney, Samuel had become friendly with Isaac Simmons (or Simmonds), a villainous fellow Jew from London who had managed to find himself a place in the small band of convict watchmen or constables set up to combat the rising crime rate in the colony.

Simmons, alias 'Hikey' Bull, was about sixteen years Samuel's senior. He had been sentenced to death at the Old Bailey in February 1797, for waylaying and robbing a man near Fenchurch Street, but the sentence was commuted to transportation for life, and he reached Sydney Cove in March 1801, about nine months before Samuel.

As a constable, he left much to be desired. He kept the company of suspicious characters, and in May 1803 was taken to court for beating a law-breaker with his wooden staff. But on that occasion he escaped with a warning, and so was still a member of the constabulary when Samuel's crime took place – though not for very long afterwards.

The affair which led to Simmons's downfall – and to the attempted execution of Joseph Samuel – began on the evening of 25 August, when the home of Mary Breeze, a woman living in Back Row (later Phillip Street), was broken into and a writing-desk containing money and other articles stolen.

Constable Joseph Luker, to whom the crime was reported, immediately suspected that Simmons and his companions were the culprits. He told the victim that later that night, when he went on duty, he would have a look round in the brush behind the houses, where he expected to catch them in the act of moving the stolen property. But the following morning Luker was found dead at the edge of a rough track. He was shockingly mutilated and had the guard of his own cutlass buried in his brain.

Near the body lay the wheel of a barrow, the carriage of which – apparently bloodstained – was found outside the home of Sarah Laurence (or Lawrence), on the opposite corner of Back Row from Mary Breeze's house. These discoveries led to the immediate apprehension of William Bladders – a man who had spent the previous night at that house – together with a number of other suspicious characters, including Joseph Samuel.

An examination of Luker's body revealed the extent of his injuries, causing shock and revulsion throughout the colony. As the *Sydney Gazette*, Australia's first newspaper, reported:

On the head of the deceased were counted Sixteen

Stabs and Contusions; the left ear was nearly divided; on the left side of the head were four wounds, and several others on the back of it.

The wretch who buried the iron guard of the cutlass in the head of the unfortunate man had seized the weapon by the blade, and levelled the dreadful blow with such fatal force, as to rivet the plate in the Skull, to a depth of more than an inch and a half.

The coroner's inquest was held the same day, and lasted five hours. It resulted in a verdict of wilful murder against William Bladders and some other person or persons unknown. Bladders was therefore committed to close custody, while several other men were detained on suspicion.

Two days after this, the stolen desk was discovered in the brush behind Back Row, about two hundred yards from the home of Mary Breeze and three hundred yards from the place where Luker's body had been found. There were several traces of blood on the top of it and its contents were missing.

That day, too, Joseph Luker was buried, following a procession in which all of his fellow constables took part. Of the four who lowered his coffin into the grave, one was Isaac Simmons.

The following day the prisoners appeared before the Lieutenant-Governor and magistrates of the colony for examination. The first was a man named Brown, who denied that he had been involved in the crime; he was remanded for further examination. Joseph Samuel ('Samuels', according to the *Gazette's* reports of the case) and a friend of his named Richard Jackson were then brought forward.

These likewise denied any involvement in the affair, but were confronted with evidence that two men – one strongly resembling Samuel – had been seen at the back of Mary Breeze's garden about six o'clock on the evening of the 25th. They, however, persisted in their denials, both declaring that they had been at the home of Isaac Simmons from 6.10 p.m. until after eight o'clock, when they went home to bed.

Simmons himself had been regarded with suspicion from the start, but had so far not been apprehended. But now he, too, was interrogated, and gave the Bench cause to think that he should also be taken into custody. So he, Samuel and Jackson were all ordered into close confinement, the two Jews being lodged in a cell together.

The examinations then continued, with William Bladders and another detainee, Thomas Hescott, being returned to prison, and a third man, James Driver, being remanded on suspicion. Four others were ordered to be released.

The next day, on being brought before the Bench again, Simmons informed the magistrate John Harris – who was also Surgeon to the New South Wales Corps, and had himself inspected Luker's body – that he had received an intimation concerning the robbery from Samuel, whom he believed wished to be admitted evidence for the Crown.

When Samuel was questioned, he at first denied this, but soon began to incriminate himself. He then asked if he could be accepted as a Crown witness after all, in order to obtain immunity from prosecution. The Bench agreed to this request, and the prisoner, while denying all knowledge of the murder, admitted that he had been involved in the crime at Mary Breeze's house. He said that the only other person who had taken part was John Russell, a man not so far detained.

John Harris demanded to know what he had done with the stolen money, reminding Samuel that his security would be withdrawn if he did not disclose all the circumstances of the crime. Samuel agreed to show him, and on being taken out into the brush behind Back Row, began to reveal various places of concealment. During the course of the search all of the stolen property was recovered, apart from some copper coins.

In the meantime, John Russell had been found and taken into custody.

But the Bench did not believe that Samuel's account was true, for other evidence appeared to belie his claim that Richard Jackson was innocent. This disbelief proved to be fully justified a day later, when Jackson made a voluntary confession, stating that he had been a principal in the crime, and that Samuel and Russell had been his accomplices. He afterwards led attendants out into the brush and showed them where the stolen desk had been forced open and the missing copper coins buried.

Faced with this fresh development, Samuel admitted that he had given false evidence the day before, explaining that he had done so because he had a particular regard for Jackson. By this declaration, he invalidated his testimony and so forfeited his chance of avoiding prosecution.

A few days later, Jackson was given an opportunity to be admitted evidence for the Crown in Samuel's place, and accepted the terms that were offered to him. Samuel and Russell were then committed for trial.

On 21 September, they appeared before the Sydney Criminal Court, charged with breaking and entering the dwelling-house of Mary Breeze, and stealing therefrom a writing-desk containing fifty dollars, three guineas, two gold coins together valued at four pounds, and a number of other articles. Samuel pleaded guilty, Russell not guilty. The case then proceeded against the latter, but proved not to be very substantial. As the *Sydney Gazette* reported:

Richard Jackson ... on oath declared that Samuels had with himself pre-concerted the Robbery, that on the aforesaid evening they observed Breeze to be out, and formed a design of carrying their intention into execution; they accidentally met (Russell) about dusk in the evening, to whom they made known what they were about to do, and proposed to him to assist them in it, to which he agreed. Samuels and the deponent went round to the back paling, leaving (Russell) as a watch in front of the house, to warn them of approaching danger, but that he never saw him after until he was himself in custody.

Asked whether it had been intended that Russell should have an equal share of the proceeds, the witness said that as they had not seen him after he had been left to keep watch for them, he and Samuel had resolved to give him nothing. In answer to a further question, he said he could not say positively that Russell had been present on any earlier occasion on which the plan to rob Mary Breeze had been discussed.

Besides being uncorroborated, Jackson's evidence was challenged by Sarah Laurence, who told the court that on the evening in question the prisoner had been to her house, at her own request, to cut some wood for her. She had not seen him outside before sending over for him, she said.

In view of all this, John Russell was acquitted.

Two days later, William Bladders and Isaac Simmons appeared for trial in the same court, charged with the wilful murder of Joseph Luker. They both denied the offence.

In this case, evidence was given that Bladders had had blood on his legs, feet and hat on the morning of the murder – which he accounted for by saying that he had assisted in the slaughter of a pig – and that the wheel-barrow's bloodstained carriage was found at the house in which he had spent the night.

As for Simmons, it was stated that he had been up and about much earlier than usual that morning (by about 5.30 a.m., when the body was found, in fact); that he had tried to remove spots of blood from the stolen writing-desk after its discovery, and that a shirt and three handkerchiefs stained with blood had been found in his possession.

But the Crown's case was by no means conclusive, for two witnesses told the court that Bladders had spent the whole night of 25 August in their company at the home of Sarah Laurence, and others supported his claim that he had been involved in killing a pig the following morning. Simmons explained the blood on his handkerchiefs by saying that he often suffered from nosebleeds, and said the blood on his shirt must have come from a fish he had cleaned or a duck stolen by Samuel which he had killed. Both men were acquitted.

Samuel, the only person convicted in connection with this affair, was sentenced to death, and the following Monday morning, 26 September, he and another condemned man were taken by cart to the place of execution, which was then near the village of Brickfield Hill in Lower George Street. It was reported that they both conducted themselves with 'becoming decency'.

At the gallows the Reverend Samuel Marsden, a minister of the Anglican Church, performed 'the duties of his function' for the other prisoner, a thief named James Hardwicke. He then turned to Samuel – who, being Jewish, had been prepared by one of his own faith – and questioned him about the murder of Joseph Luker. At this, Samuel said that while confined in a cell together he and Isaac Simmons had exchanged an oath, binding themselves to 'secrecy and silence' in respect of anything which they might then disclose to each other. What happened next was recounted in the *Gazette's* report as follows:

Conjured by that GOD before whom he was shortly to appear, not to advance any thing in his latter moments that would endanger his salvation, he now repeated with an air of firmness what he had before declared; and appearing deeply imprest with a becoming sense of his approaching end, appealed to Heaven to bear him testimony, that Simmonds had, under the influence of the oath by which they were reciprocally bound, acknowledged to him that Luker had accidentally surprised him with the desk belonging to Mary Breeze; and that he, in consequence thereof, had 'knocked him down, and given him a topper for luck!' adding at the same time, that if he had not been kept in the dark with respect to the concealment of the money that had been taken out of it, that catastrophe never would have happened; but as it was, that he would hang 500 Christians to save himself.

Simmons was among the spectators. He had by now lost his position as constable, and had been put to hard labour, as evidence given before the magistrates showed that he had been harbouring infamous characters in his house and encouraging them in their unlawful activities. He had therefore been brought along to Brickfield Hill deliberately, so that he could be present at the death of one of them.

On hearing himself accused of Luker's murder – of which, in spite of his acquittal, he was still widely suspected – he began to make noisy interruptions, trying to prevent the speaker continuing. But Samuel went on with his declaration, speaking with mildness and composure, and before long 'the feelings of the multitude burst forth into invective' against the person he was denouncing. Simmons must then have been in danger of being attacked, but it seems that no assault actually occurred.

Shortly afterwards, as the condemned men stood waiting to be hanged, a reprieve arrived for Hardwicke and was announced by the Provost Marshal. Samuel then spent the last moments before the cart was driven off in earnest and fervent prayer, unaware that what was in store for him was very different from the usual fate of prisoners left for execution.

Eventually, the hangman went to work. Samuel was left hanging from the gallows, until suddenly the rope broke and he fell to the ground. Still alive, he went on lying there, motionless, until the cart was brought back. He was then held up on both sides while another rope was used in place of the broken one. But when he was hanged again this new rope began to unravel, and soon the culprit's legs trailed along the ground, leaving his body only partially suspended.

By this time the spectators were greatly moved, and some began to say that the hand of Providence was at work on Samuel's behalf. But the condemned man, now unconscious, was lifted onto other men's shoulders, so that the hangman could make yet another attempt to carry out his sentence – using a third rope. Samuel was then gently lowered, so that he could be left to hang – but this rope, like the first, broke when it took his weight, and he again fell to the ground.

Halting the execution, the Provost Marshal hurried off to see the Governor of the colony. When he returned, he announced that Samuel had now been granted a reprieve, a piece of news which the crowd received with joy.

Samuel himself was incapable of understanding what had happened, and was only able to utter incoherences for some time afterwards. But within a day or two, by means of surgical assistance, the use of his faculties was restored.

One of the ropes which had been used to hang him was afterwards tested. It was found to be strong enough to support seven weights, each of 56 lb, even after two of its three strands had been cut. So it could only have been defective at the point at which it actually broke.

On the day following Samuel's abortive execution, Isaac Simmons went back to his workgang. Just twelve days after that, the *Gazette* reported:

Yesterday Isaac Simmonds was brought in from the Battery at George's Head, and punished with 50 lashes in front of the gaol, for disorderly conduct, neglect of work, and being refractory. In the evening he was returned to the Battery, there to remain till further Orders.

There was nothing unusual about this, for such punishments were inflicted for even the most trivial offences. Simmons may well have been flogged on other occasions as well before he was finally released.

*

Samuel's reprieve must have been followed by a commutation of sentence, for no further attempt was made to hang him, and sometime during the next year or so he was transferred to the penal settlement at Kings Town, Newcastle, seventy-five miles away. There he got into trouble again, as the *Sydney Gazette* of 18 August 1805 informs us:

A robbery was three weeks since perpetrated at King's Town, Newcastle on the property of John Green, his chest having been wrenched open. Joseph Samuels was taken up on suspicion, & after much evasion, consented to acknowledge the fact upon certain conditions; and at length confessed himself the principal and criminated another as an accomplice.

The latter admitted that he had received the property from Samuels, and secreted the whole among the sand on the beach. The spot of interment, however, could not be found, and such mode of treatment was adopted by the Gentleman in command as the heinous nature of the offence required.

Samuel was undoubtedly flogged, probably far more severely than Simmons had been. But, like John Smith, he was quite incorrigible, and a few months later he absconded from public labour. This led to his name being included, with those of nine other escaped convicts, in a public notice inserted in the same newspaper on 22 December.

We do not know how he lived while he was on the run. Perhaps he found refuge in the home of a free settler, working to pay for his keep, or perhaps – like many other fugitives – he took to the woods and led a life of depredation. At any rate, he succeeded in avoiding recapture for the next three months. But then, on 1 April 1806, he and seven other escaped convicts put out to sea from Newcastle in an open boat, for an unknown destination.

The Government boat *Resource* arrived in Newcastle two days later, and was sent out to search for them. But no trace of them was found, and it was assumed that Samuel and his companions had all drowned during a tempest on their second night at sea.

*

Isaac Simmons remained a convict until 31 January 1818, when he was granted a free pardon, almost twenty-one years after his conviction at the Old Bailey. He then stayed on in Sydney as a free settler, and is known to have had other convicts assigned to him as servants on two occasions.

He died, aged about sixty-eight, on 13 October 1833, and was buried in the Jewish part of the Old Devonshire Street Cemetery.

5. A dream that came true

John Lee was a twenty-year-old servant convicted of the brutal murder of his employer. Like Joseph Samuel, he survived three attempts to hang him, and became known as 'the man they could not hang'. It was the only case in which an abortive execution took place in this country after the introduction of the long drop, so it is justifiably still famous over a hundred years later.

Miss Emma Keyse, the victim of the murder, lived in a two-storey thatched cottage at Babbacombe, near Torquay. She was a wealthy woman of sixty-eight, a member of the local gentry, well liked in the district. Besides Lee, she had three other servants: two elderly sisters, Eliza and Jane Neck, who had been in her household for forty years, and a young cook named Elizabeth Harris, who was Lee's half-sister.

John Lee had first entered Miss Keyse's service in a minor capacity at the age of fourteen or fifteen, having been born and brought up in the nearby village of Abbotskerswell. He stayed with her for eighteen months, then went off to join the Royal Navy and spent the next year or two at sea. But a bout of pneumonia brought his new career to an end, and not long afterwards he was given a sentence of six months' hard labour for stealing silver from a Colonel Brownlow of Torquay, by whom he was then employed.

It was the only time that he had been in trouble so far, and Miss Keyse, who had always found him to be honest and trustworthy, later offered to take him back into her service, provided he promised not to give her any cause for anxiety. By this time Lee had almost completed his sentence, and was pleased to have an opportunity to live down what had happened. He thus returned to her household on his release from prison.

This time, however, he soon became discontented. He saw himself as having to give a man's service for a boy's pay, and resented being unable to better himself. To make things worse, his employer began to find fault with his work, and suddenly told him – after he had been back with her for nine months – that she was going to reduce his wages from 2s 6d to 2s a week. John Lee naturally harboured ill-feeling as a result of all this, and was several times heard to utter threats against her.

During the early hours of 15 November 1884, Miss Keyse was murdered in her own house, after the servants had all apparently gone to bed. The doors had already been bolted, the windows checked, and Jane Neck had made her employer a cup of cocoa, as usual, before retiring at 12.40 a.m. Miss Keyse had then changed into a nightgown and a small woollen jacket, and had drunk some of the cocoa before her murderer struck.

It was a callous crime, a deliberate and savage act. Besides battering his victim over the head with a heavy instrument, the culprit cut her throat, inflicting a wound so deep that the vertebrae of her neck were notched. He afterwards moved the body from the hall – where the attack had taken place – to the dining-room, and there made an attempt to burn it. He also started fires in other parts of the house.

Unaware that anything out of the ordinary was happening, the three female servants slept on – as did John Lee himself, according to his own account. But sometime between three and four o'clock, Elizabeth Harris woke up and smelt something burning. She roused the Neck sisters, and Eliza went downstairs through dense smoke. It was then that Miss Keyse's body was found, with fire smouldering all round it.

John Lee had by this time come out of the pantry where he slept, and Eliza – shocked though she must have been – had sufficient presence of mind to ask him to go to their nearest neighbour, the landlord of the Carey Arms Public House, for assistance. But instead of going at once, he stayed to help Jane down the stairs,

213

holding her round the waist. And even then – after Jane had also asked him to go – he went with some reluctance.

When he finally raised the alarm, help began to arrive. The badly burnt corpse of his employer was then carried outside and the fire was extinguished. During the investigation which followed it soon became clear that the fire had been started deliberately, with the use of paraffin, and it was suspected that the person responsible had been trying to burn down the whole house.

There were no signs of a forced entry, and nothing of value was missing. A hatchet normally used for chopping wood and a sharp knife found in a drawer in the pantry were both found to be bloodstained; so, too, was an oil-can kept in a pantry cupboard. A coat and a pair of trousers which John Lee had worn on the night of the murder both smelt strongly of paraffin and were blood-stained in various places; one of his socks, besides smelling of paraffin, had human hair attached to it – and this was found to be similar to the hair of the victim. Another bloodstain was found on Jane Neck's night-gown, at a point where Lee, in helping her down the stairs, had taken hold of her arm.

Lee said that on the morning of 15 November he had heard no sound until he was roused from sleep by the shouting of the other servants. He tried to account for the blood on his clothes by saying that he had cut his arm while breaking a window to let out the smoke. He also tried to mislead the police by pretending that Miss Keyse had been his best friend. But all of these claims were found to be false, and Lee was charged with murder.

The brutality with which the crime had been committed caused much ill-feeling towards him, and his three-day trial at Exeter, beginning on 2 February 1885, was followed with great interest. The prosecution's case was overwhelming, and the defence could do little to help him beyond suggesting that Elizabeth Harris, who was pregnant, may have secretly entertained the child's father on the night of 14 November, and that *he* may have committed the crime as he left her in the early hours of the morning. The jury took only forty minutes to find the prisoner guilty.

Mr Justice Manisty, in passing sentence of death, described the murder of Miss Keyse as one of the most cruel and barbarous murders ever committed. He remarked upon the calm and collected demeanour which Lee had maintained throughout the trial, saying that such behaviour was not impossible to a man who could commit so terrible a crime. Warning the prisoner that he could not hope for mercy, he exhorted him to spend his few remaining days on earth in preparation for the next world.

To this, however, the condemned man replied, 'The reason, my lord, why I am so calm and collected is because I trust in my Lord, and He knows I am innocent.'

He was then removed from the courtroom and taken back to Exeter Prison, where he remained in the condemned cell until 23 February, when the sentence was due to be carried out. On the night of the 22nd, he was as impassive as ever, and after writing some letters and receiving the sacrament, he settled down to sleep. He then had a strange dream, in which he was on a scaffold, waiting to be hanged, but the drop failed to work. Three attempts were made to hang him, and each was unsuccessful. In the morning, he told the warders in his cell about this dream, but no importance was attached to it until later.

Executions in Britain were no longer carried out in public, and the use of the long drop made hanging more humane than the methods which had been used before. But there were still occasional mishaps, resulting in frightful convulsions after the condemned had fallen through the trap. One could never be sure that one of these incidents was not about to occur.

At Exeter, the place of execution was the prison coach-house, where two trapdoors in the floor covered a pit about eleven feet deep. James Berry, the hangman, had inspected it two days earlier and found it to be in working order, though he suggested that thicker doors with stronger ironwork should be used in future. He evidently saw no reason to expect any difficulty in hanging John Lee.

Just before eight o'clock that morning, the condemned man was pinioned in his cell and led out to the drop. There his legs were strapped together, a white cap pulled down over his face, and the rope placed round his neck and adjusted. The hangman asked him whether he had anything to say, and Lee replied in the negative. Then, as the Chaplain concluded the Burial Service, the hangman pulled the lever operating the trapdoors. But, as in Lee's dream, the doors failed to open. The prisoner just went on standing there.

In the tense moments which followed, Berry moved the lever to and fro with great force, but to no avail. The trapdoors remained firmly closed. Lee, who had not uttered a word throughout this ordeal, had therefore to be taken from the drop, and an axe, a saw and a plane brought so that adjustments could be made. Within a few minutes the drop was tested and found to work satisfactorily. But when a second attempt was made to hang the condemned man, the result was the same as before. The doors failed to open.

By now, the Governor, the Under-Sheriff, the hangman and other officials present were all in a state of consternation. Warders tried to force the trapdoors open by stamping on them, but this was likewise to no avail. So Lee was again removed from the drop and this time taken to the prison basement while further adjustments were made. A third attempt to hang him, after several more minutes had elapsed, was no more successful than the others. The trapdoors remained closed.

The Reverend John Pitkin, the Prison Chaplain, later recalled in his memoirs how at this moment he and all the other officials stood there, 'mentally paralysed by the hopelessness of the task we were all by law expected to perform. For the third time I had concluded the service; for the third time the prisoner had felt the agonies of death; for the third time the responsible officers failed in their attempt to execute the man.' The Under-Sheriff was thus placed in a terrible dilemma – from which he was suddenly extricated by the Chaplain himself.

Acting on the advice of the Prison Surgeon, Mr Pitkin announced that he would remain at the place of execution no longer. This ensured that the hanging would be postponed, as it could not be carried out in his absence. Lee was therefore taken back to his cell, where the Chaplain stayed with him for some time.

In spite of the agony which he must have suffered, Lee continued to bear up, and even refused the stimulant for which the Governor had sent. He told the Chaplain about his dream of the previous night, which now seemed to have come true in every respect. But he was not at all grateful that he was still alive, and said he wanted the sentence to be carried out.

The news that Lee had survived three attempts to hang him caused great excitement among the crowds which had gathered outside the jail, and before long newspaper offices were besieged by people wanting to know whether there had been any further developments in the case.

That afternoon, Lee's sentence was respited by the Home Secretary, Sir William Harcourt. It was afterwards commuted to life imprisonment.

Lee was not informed of this commutation at the time, as it was thought advisable that the news should be withheld from him until the official notification arrived at the prison. He was still in ignorance of it the following day, for in a letter which he then wrote to his sister he said that he was still hoping to be hanged, even though he believed the failure of the drop to have been 'a miracle worked by the Lord'. Presumably, the notification arrived later the same day.

It was generally accepted that the failure of the drop in this very unusual case was due to the trapdoors having become swollen with rain the night before. But the hangman, who only admitted having made *two* attempts to hang the prisoner, put it down to the defects which he had already pointed out.

As he wrote in his report of the incident:

I am of opinion that the ironwork catches of the trap-doors were not strong enough for the purpose, that the woodwork of the doors should have been about three or four times as heavy, and with iron-work to correspond, so that when a man of Lee's weight was placed upon the doors the iron catches would not have become locked, as I feel sure they did on this occasion, but would respond readily.

There were also, inevitably, those who – like Lee himself – believed that the failure was due to Divine intervention, and said it proved that the prisoner had been wrongfully convicted.

Whatever the reason for it, the Home Secretary took the view that the abortive execution left only one course open to him, as a further attempt to hang the offender would inspire horror and compassion among the public at large. Lee's sentence had therefore to be commuted, whether he liked it or not, and this was done without delay.

But it was not a popular decision. It was attacked in various quarters, and bitterly resented by friends of the victim. Lee, for all his suffering, was still a cold-blooded murderer, and to many people the idea of allowing him to escape the death penalty was intolerable.

John Lee served twenty-two years in jail: a lot longer than most life sentences. No doubt the atrocity of his crime was taken into account each time the question of his release arose, but it was also said that he had repeatedly uttered threats against his half-sister, Elizabeth Harris, for giving evidence for the prosecution at his trial.

At any rate, he was finally discharged from Portland, in Dorset, on 17 December 1907, and went back to Abbotskerswell to stay with his widowed mother. The news of his return brought newspaper reporters to the village, and by the end of the month *Lloyd's Weekly News* began publishing his life story in weekly instalments.

The Man They Could Not Hang, probably written with the assistance of a journalist, was republished in book form shortly afterwards. It did not give a credible account of the case, for Lee's determination to go on protesting his innocence made this impossible. But it was still an enthralling tale to anyone unfamiliar with the known facts, and so became quite popular. The sale of the story enabled Lee to live well for several months.

A year after his release, the Babbacombe murderer married Jessie Augusta Bulleid, the chief nurse of the female mental ward of Newton Abbott Workhouse. The couple moved to London – where Lee made his living as a barman for a while – and had two children. But in February 1912, Mrs Lee had to apply to the Lambeth Guardians for assistance, her husband having by this time left her without making any provision for the family's maintenance. It was rumoured that he had gone to Australia with another woman.

A few years after his disappearance, a silent film based on his life story was released, and it has been suggested that Lee may have returned to Britain in order to travel round the country with it. This would have been quite in character with him, for he had previously made the most of his reputation. But there appears to be no evidence that he actually did so – or that he ever returned for any other purpose, either.

He may, in fact, have died in Australia during the First World War, as newspapers of the time reported. But it is generally believed that he settled in the United States, dying in Milwaukee in 1933, at the age of sixty-eight.

Whatever became of him, we may be sure that he vanished into obscurity of his own accord. It also seems likely that he kept out of trouble for the rest of his life, for had he not done so his identity would soon have been discovered.

6. Hanged man lived to be proved innocent

While John Lee was serving his life sentence in England, another famous case of survival occurred, this time in the United States. Will Purvis, a farmer's son from Devils Bend, near Columbia in south Mississippi, was convicted of murdering one of the owners of a neighbouring farm. But he was innocent of the crime, and was later exonerated by another ınan's confession. This, however, was not until many years after his abortive execution had taken place.

In 1893, when the case began, the black people of that part of Mississippi were being terrorized by a secret organization called the White Caps, which had been set up with the avowed intention of upholding law and order. Purvis, then aged twenty, had recently become a member, and was thus present when a small band seized and flogged Sam Waller, a farmhand employed by two brothers named Will and Jim Buckley.

The incident was just one of many acts of violence for which the White Caps were responsible. But Will

Buckley, who was himself a member, was outraged by it, and made known his intention to have charges brought against those concerned. With this object in mind, he, his brother and Sam Waller all rode into Columbia to give evidence about the affair before a grand jury. Afterwards, as they made their way home, Will Buckley was shot dead in an ambush, his killers escaping from the scene of the crime.

Jim Buckley claimed that Will Purvis had been one of the ambushers, and said he was certain that it was he who had fired the fatal shot. Sheriff Irving Otho Magee and several deputies therefore went to the Purvis family's farm and arrested him, the accused man assuming that a mistake of some sort had been made and that he would soon be released. Instead, he was charged with murder.

The crime, which had taken place on 22 June 1893, aroused intense feeling among the inhabitants of south Mississippi. Many people who had been indifferent to crimes against the blacks felt that the murder of a white man could not be tolerated. There were even fears that an attempt might be made to rescue the prisoner. So when Purvis appeared for trial in Columbia on 4 August, the courthouse was guarded by the state militia, and spectators were allowed to take guns into the building.

The case against the prisoner was not very strong, for the prosecution had little evidence other than that of Jim Buckley. Against this, the defence called witnesses to testify that Purvis had been at his home, five miles away, at the time of the shooting, and for some hours either side of it. But in the atmosphere in which the trial was held, their evidence was seen as unconvincing.

'There were revolvers, shotguns and rifles on every hand,' one of the defence attorneys was to recall many years later. 'The court, jury and the people at large seemed obsessed with the feeling that this reign of terror must be curbed. The strain and stress was so great that an acquittal seemed impossible, a conviction inevitable.'

It was therefore no surprise when the jury returned a verdict of guilty, and Will Purvis went back to jail under sentence of death.

His hanging was delayed for several months by an unsuccessful appeal to the State Supreme Court, but was finally fixed for 7 February 1894. On that day, excited crowds gathered before a heavily guarded scaffold outside the courthouse in Columbia, and waited to see justice take its course. Shortly before noon, the condemned man, now aged twenty-one, was brought from his cell and placed on the trapdoor, white-faced and nervous.

Sheriff Magee, assisted by three deputies, made the final preparations for the execution, then asked Purvis whether he had anything to say. With his wrists and ankles bound, and the rope round his neck, the prisoner made a short speech to the crowds, saying that he was innocent of the murder an that there were people present who could save him if they wanted to. But nobody tried to save him, and a black cap was placed over his head. The Reverend James G. Sibley, pastor of the Columbia Methodist Church, prayed loudly as the moment of death appeared to be drawing near.

As all was now ready, the Sheriff took up a hatchet and severed a stay rope holding the trapdoor in position. The trap then opened and Will Purvis fell through it. But to the horror of all who were present, the rope failed to hold him and he landed heavily on the ground beneath the scaffold. Apparently, the knot of the halter had come undone as it took his weight, though some accounts state that the noose actually slipped over his head. Either way, it was a shocking mishap.

For a few moments, Purvis lay on the ground where he had fallen, unconscious but not seriously hurt. When he came to he was lifted back up the steps of the scaffold, so that a second attempt could be made to carry out his sentence. But at this point Mr Sibley and other influential citizens intervened, claiming that what had happened was an act of God – and a sign that the condemned man was innocent.

Before long, the crowds which had come to watch the hanging were on the prisoner's side, and in a show of hands declared themselves against the idea that he should be made to suffer again. The Sheriff then agreed to postpone the execution while he sought the instructions of the District Attorney. So Purvis was again taken back to jail.

The Sheriff's failure to carry out the execution placed the District Attorney, James H. Neville, under an obligation to have the prisoner arraigned for re-sentencing before the court where he had been tried. It also raised serious doubts about his guilt in Magee's own mind, as the Sheriff pointed out in his report to the State Governor, John M. Stone, the following day.

As he himself saw no reason to question the jury's verdict, Stone refused to commute Purvis's sentence. But the re-sentencing, followed by three more unsuccessful appeals to the Supreme Court, prevented a second attempt being carried out for nearly two years.

Purvis spent much of that time in jail in Hattiesburg, but the last five months in the town of Purvis, where his parents were now living. It was while he was in Purvis that the Supreme Court turned down his third appeal and set 12 December 1895 as the new date for his execution.

But in Purvis the condemned man had friends and relatives who were willing to resort to desperate means in order to save him, and a few days before the law was due to take its course he was warned to be ready to make his escape.

That night, about nine o'clock, Purvis pretended to be asleep as the guards made their last inspection, then got up and looked out through the window. He heard, in the distance, the sound of somebody rapping on a log with a paint brush, and recognized this as the signal for a rescue to be made.

At that moment, two men walked up to the Sheriff's Office, pushed rifles through the window and warned those inside to be quiet. The occupants offered no resistance, and the two men kept them under guard while others entered the building and set the prisoner free. Purvis left the town on a mule which had been waiting outside for him.

He remained at liberty, with a price on his head, for over a year, sometimes staying with relatives and sometimes living rough. He later declared that those days were the most miserable in his whole life, and that he sometimes wished his friends had not been so hasty in rescuing him. But then, in February 1897, the new State Governor, Anselm J. McLaurin, offered to show leniency if the fugitive gave himself up.

Purvis did so, and spent almost two years in a convict camp after his sentence had been commuted to life imprisonment. Then, on 19 December 1898, he was granted a full pardon in response to public pressure.

*

After his release he went back to working for his father, and later acquired a 120-acre farm of his own seven miles north of Purvis. On 27 September 1899 – his twenty-seventh birthday – he married Sarah Boone, the daughter of a Baptist minister. They had eleven children.

Purvis's case became news again in 1917, when a sixty-year-old farmer named Joe Beard confessed on his deathbed that he had taken part in the ambush in which Will Buckley had been killed, and named Louis Thornhill, a man already dead, as the person who had fired the fatal shot.

He revealed that Thornhill and he, both members of the White Caps, had been given the duty of killing both brothers after they gave evidence before the grand jury. But when Thornhill shot Will Buckley, he (Beard) found it impossible to shoot Jim. His heart, he said, had suddenly failed him.

It was clear from Beard's confession that Purvis had been convicted in error, and three years later, on 15 March 1920, the State Legislature voted to award him $5000 compensation.

Will Purvis later gave public lectures and radio talks about his case, and his *True Life Story*, written with the assistance of Frances Williams Griffith, was published in 1935.

A respected member of the community with a keen interest in church affairs, he died in Lumberton Hospital, at the age of sixty-six, on 13 October 1938.

7. He survived the electric chair

The last of these cases is not nearly as well known as that of John Lee or Will Purvis, but it is far more recent, far more tragic – and every bit as remarkable. One imagines that opponents of the death penalty could use it to great effect in their propaganda, but so far, at least, they have not done so. It seems somehow to have escaped their attention.

The crime with which the affair started was a fairly commonplace one by American standards. On the morning of 8 November 1944, Andrew Thomas, a fifty-four-year-old drug-store owner, was found dead at the back of his home in St Martinville, a small town in Louisiana. He had been shot once in the head and four times in the body during the course of a struggle, and the contents of his pockets had been stolen.

As Thomas had had no known enemies, it seemed safe to assume that robbery had been the motive for the murder, but for some months no suspect emerged. Then, on 6 August 1945, a black youth from St Martinville was apprehended in Port Arthur, Texas, on a charge of robbery and assault and, under questioning, admitted that he had killed Thomas.

Willie Francis, aged sixteen, had worked at the Thomas Drug Store, but had taken offence when the owner reprimanded him. He confessed that on the night of the shooting he had lain in wait for Thomas and shot him when he arrived home. He had then hidden at the scene of the crime for a short while before stealing the victim's watch and wallet, the latter containing just $4. He afterwards threw away the murder weapon and sold Thomas's watch.

The youth's arrest caused little excitement in St Martinville, no doubt because it coincided with the dropping of the first atom bomb. But justice started to take its course just the same, and on 12 September, Willie Francis was brought to trial in St Martin Parish, the court appointing two attorneys to defend him.

The trial itself was uneventful, the prosecution having all the evidence it needed and the defence none at all. The prisoner watched the proceedings without showing any emotion, and on the second day was found guilty of murder. On 14 September, the judge pronounced sentence in the customary manner: 'Under Article 30 of the Criminal Code of Louisiana, I now sentence you, Willie Francis, to suffer death in the manner provided by law.'

The passing of this sentence was no mere formality, and, in spite of the prisoner's age, no commutation followed. But it was not until several months after the trial that an attempt was made to carry it out – and even then it was not done successfully. In the meantime, Willie Francis remained in his death cell, as unremorseful as ever.

The method of execution used in that state was the electric chair: a portable instrument of death which was moved from place to place as occasion demanded. For this particular execution, on 3 May 1946, it was wired up in the St Martin Parish Jail, though the condemned youth had been confined in a different parish.

Willie Francis, now seventeen, was strapped into the chair and the electrodes were fitted into place in the normal way. But when the switch controlling the electric current was thrown, it quickly became apparent that it was not working properly. Francis, after squirming for a moment or two, was heard shouting from under the hood, 'Take it off! Take it off! I'm smothering!'

The switch was then released, the straps undone, and the witnesses sat spellbound as Willie Francis, who should now have been dead, straightened himself up. A telephone call to the State Governor resulted in a six-day reprieve being granted, and the condemned youth walked unaided from the jail as police officers took him back to the parish of Iberia.

On arrival at the jail there, he told attendants that he had not been nervous at the prospect of imminent death because the Lord had been with him. Before being strapped into the chair he had been thinking about going to Heaven and wondering what Hell was like, he said. He also claimed that at the moment the switch was thrown he had felt a current of electricity, which 'tickled him a bit, but did not hurt much'.

With news services and newspapers all over the country clamouring for details of this unprecedented mishap, embarrassed officials pointed out that the chair had been tested and found to be in working order before the execution was attempted. Later, after it had been taken to Baton Rouge for examination, the Warden of the State Penitentiary expressed the view that its failure had probably been caused by a wire burning out. Other officials, however, put it down to a *loose* wire.

The accident, whatever its cause, prompted many people to write to the State Governor, pleading for the youth's life to be spared, and a St Martinville attorney named Bertrand DeBlanc began a tireless struggle to achieve this end through the courts.

DeBlanc contended that Francis had already been electrocuted, as ordered in the Governor's death warrant, and could not legally be subjected to the same punishment again. When he failed to obtain a writ of habeas corpus from District Judge James D. Simon (who had also been the trial judge), he appealed to the State Supreme Court. The Acting Governor then granted a new reprieve, staying the execution until 7 June.

DeBlanc asked the Supreme Court to overturn Judge Simon's decision, arguing that a second attempt to carry out the death sentence would place Francis in double jeopardy, in contravention of the United States Constitution. But the Court held that the District Judge had been within his rights in refusing a writ of habeas corpus, and accepted that it had no authority to commute the prisoner's sentence. The appeal was therefore dismissed.

The case was then taken to the State Pardon Board, before which DeBlanc argued that the State had carried out its duty in respect of the sentence, and that Willie Francis had been saved from death by an act of God. The Board, by a unanimous decision, refused to recommend clemency.

DeBlanc then announced that an appeal would be made to the US Supreme Court, and obtained a further reprieve, this one worded in such a way that it would last until a decision on the appeal had been reached. The new petition was filed by a Washington attorney, James S. Wright, asking the Court to review a plea of 'cruel and unusual punishment', as well as double jeopardy, stating that Francis had already been through 'the most gruelling experience known to man'.

It was announced on 10 June that the Court would not review the case, but this turned out to be a mistake on the part of one of its officials. The following day, it was rectified with an announcement that the case would be heard during the Court's new term, beginning in October.

'I think we have a good chance in the Supreme Court,' Bertrand DeBlanc told representatives of the press. 'I'm going to Washington in October. I still say that Francis's delivery from the electric chair was an act of God.'

All this time, Willie Francis remained in his death cell in the New Iberia Parish Jail. He spent a lot of his time praying and reading his prayer book, and had a Catholic priest visiting him every day.

The Supreme Court did not reach its decision until 13 January 1947, when it ruled by five votes to four that a second attempt to carry out the execution would not be unconstitutional. One of the judges supporting this view made it known that he was personally in favour of clemency, but believed that the Court had no right to prevent any state taking its pound of flesh.

The Weekly Messenger, a local newspaper, reported that this verdict was seen as just in St Martinville, where, it claimed, the majority of inhabitants expected 'to see Francis pay with his life for his cold blooded, premeditated murder'.

Wright then went back to ask the Supreme Court to reconsider its decision. This time he argued that the opinions expressed by the judges indicated that the case should be handled by Executive clemency, but that the Pardon Board's decision prevented the State Governor from commuting the sentence. The Court refused the request.

In April, Bertrand DeBlanc made a new appeal to the Pardon Board, this time producing evidence of misconduct at the abortive execution almost a year earlier. He offered an affidavit, stating that 'the executioner and other persons connected with the carrying out of the execution' had been 'so drunk that it was impossible for them to have known what they were doing'. But the Pardon Board again refused to recommend clemency, and the Acting Governor issued a new death warrant, ordering the execution to be carried out on 9 May.

An application for a new trial was refused; a fresh appeal to the State Supreme Court was equally unsuccessful. Willie Francis, now eighteen, accepted the news calmly, saying that he would wear his best clothes for the occasion.

'Ain't going to wear no beat-up pants to see the Lord,' he said. 'Been busy talking my way into Heaven for the past year. Them folks expecting me to come in style.'

On 8 May the question of misconduct at the abortive execution was raised in the US Supreme Court, in support of yet another appeal. This time, James S. Wright, repeating the allegations which had been made previously, stated in his petition:

'The scene was a disgraceful and inhuman exhibition, that as soon as the switch controlling the current was taken off, the drunken executioner cursed Francis and told him he would be back to finish electrocuting him, and if the electricity did not kill him he would kill him with a rock.'

While accepting that 'grave new allegations' had been made, the Court denied Wright's plea for a writ of habeas corpus, and likewise turned down an appeal by DeBlanc to overturn the decision of the Supreme Court of Louisiana.

The following morning, Francis, who did not know about these latest attempts to save his life, told DeBlanc to make no last-minute appeal on his behalf. He said that he was ready to die.

Shortly before noon, he was taken back to St Martin Parish Jail, where the executioner and the electric chair awaited him for the second time. With him at the end was Father Charles Hannigan, the Catholic priest who had visited him every day since the previous attempt to carry out the sentence.

Willie Francis again faced the prospect of his own

death without any apparent fear or excitement. Asked whether he had anything to say, he replied, 'Nothing at all.'

He walked his last few yards without assistance, with Father Hannigan preceding him.

The executioner, Grady Jarrett, threw the switch at 12.05 p.m., and again a minute later. This time there was no mishap, and at 12.10 the luckless young murderer was pronounced dead.

SOURCES OF INFORMATION

The Genial Schemer's Tragic Mistake

Most of the information used in this story has been taken from contemporary newspaper reports published in *The Times, Illustrated Police News, Reynolds's Newspaper,* the *Daily News, Daily Mirror, Weekly Dispatch* and *News of the World*, but certain details have been taken from birth, marriage or death certificates. Other sources used were short accounts of the case published in *Science and the Criminal* (1911) and *A Scientist in the Criminal Courts* (1945), both by C. Ainsworth Mitchell, and *Inquest* (1941), the memoirs of the Coroner S. Ingleby Oddie. W.H. Speer's account, in *The Secret History of Great Crimes* (1929), seems to be largely a work of imagination, while others by Norman Lucas (in *The Laboratory Detectives*, 1971) and Leonard Gribble (*They Came to Kill*, 1979) contain no new information on the case, and also cannot be recommended from the point of view of accuracy.

The Strange Affair of the Lyons Mail

In this case, all of the information has been taken from *The Lyons Mail* (1945) by Sir Charles Oman, though the conclusion reached is different. Accounts which argue that Lesurques was innocent include one by René Floriot in *Les Erreurs Judiciaires* (Paris, 1968), which appeared in an English translation, *When Justice Falters*, by Rayner Heppenstall in 1972.

Coldblooded Murder in a Desolate Place

The sources for this story are newspaper reports published in *The West Australian* (Perth), between 19 January and 14 June 1932, and Arthur Upfield's own account, *The Murchison Murders*, published in Sydney about 1934. Shorter accounts of the case are to be found in Eric Clegg's *Return Your Verdict* (1965) and Alan Sharpe's *Crimes That Shocked Australia* (Sydney, 1982). The latter gives further references.

Survivors of the Death Penalty

Most of the publications consulted in connection with these stories are to be found in the British Library, the Guildhall Library or the Colindale Newspaper Library, but in some cases copies had to be obtained elsewhere. Besides books, newspapers and broadsides, a small number of unpublished sources proved to be most informative. Details of these are included in the following lists:

1. Hanged – then pardoned

A Compleat Collection of Remarkable Tryals of the Most Notorious Malefactors at the Sessions-House in the Old Baily for Near Fifty Years Past (1718), II, 188– 92.

Luttrell, Narcissus: *A Brief Historical Relation of State*

Affairs, V, 623; VI, 22, 25.

Hatton, Edward: *A New View of London* (1708), I, 84–5.

Coldham, Peter Wilson: *English Convicts in Colonial America* (Polyanthos, New Orleans, 1974–6), II, 164.

Old Bailey Sessions Papers, 23–25 February 1715, 5–10 November 1716, 2–3 June 1720, 11–14 October 1721, 17–18 May 1727.

Newspapers: *The Flying-Post*, 13–15 December 1705. The *Post Boy*, 23–26 November 1706; 14–17 October 1721. The *Weekly Journal*, 26 February 1714 (-15); 30 April 1715. The *Weekly Journal or British Gazetteer*, 16 September 1721; 1 July 1727. The *Weekly Journal or Saturday's Post*, 14 May 1720; 16 September and 14 October 1721. *Applebee's*, 16 September and 14 October 1721. The *Daily Post*, 16 October 1721. The *British Journal*, 1 July 1727. The *London Journal*, 1 July 1727.

Smith's petition against transportation, in the name of John Wilson, is preserved at the Corporation of London Record Office (ref. *Small MS Box 38, no. 3*).

2. A noise from inside the coffin

Chambers, Robert: *Domestic Annals of Scotland* (1859–61), III, 500–2.

High Court Minute Book for 1724 (Scottish Record Office, ref. *JC 7/12*).

Broadsides: *The Last Speech, Confession and Warning of Margaret Dickson* and *News from Mussleburgh* (both published in Edinburgh in 1724) (National Library of Scotland).

Newspapers: The *London Journal*, 26 September 1724. *Parker's London News*, 26 October 1724.

3. A rescue at Execution Dock

Hay, Douglas (and others): *Albion's Fatal Tree* (1975), pp. 86–7, 104.

The Political State of Great Britain (1739), pp. 33–4.

The Ordinary's Account, 20 December 1738.

The Gentleman's Magazine (1738), pp. 602, 659; (1739), p. 46.

Newspapers: *Read's Weekly Journal*, 18 November 1738. The *Country Journal*, 23 December 1738. *Hooker's Weekly Miscellany*, 13 January 1739. *Old England*, 18 August 1750.

4. Three times hanged – and still he lived

Bergman, G.F.J: *The Story of Two Jewish Convicts (Australian Jewish Historical Society Journal*, March 1963).

Old Bailey Sessions Papers, 20 May 1795; 15 February 1797.

Newspapers: The *Sydney Gazette*, 28 August–9 October 1803; 18 August and 22 December 1805; 18 May 1806.

5. A dream that came true

Pitkin, Rev. John: *The Prison Cell in its Lights and Shadows* (1918), pp. 190–234.

Berry, James: *My Experiences as an Executioner* (1972 ed.), pp. 59–63.

Logan, Guy B.H.: *Rope, Knife and Chair* (1933 ed.), pp. 61–70.

Bossiney Books: *Murder in the Westcountry* (1975), pp. 101–13.

Lee, John: *The Man They Could Not Hang* (1908).

Gaute, J.H.H. & Odell, Robin: *Murder 'Whatdunit'* (1984 ed.), pp. 231–3.

The Times: 3–5 and 24 February 1885; 19 December 1907.

6. Hanged man lived to be proved innocent

Griffith, Frances Williams: *True Life Story of Will Purvis* (Purvis, Miss., 1935).

Mencken, August (ed.): *By the Neck: a Book of Hangings* (New York, 1942), pp. 49–57.

Journal of the House of Representatives, 1920 (*House Bill no. 540*).

Newspapers: *Daily Clarion-Ledger* (Jackson, Miss.), 8 February 1894. *Hattiesburg American* (Hattiesburg, Miss.), 2 November 1950. *The Clarion Ledger* (Jackson, Miss.), 26 June 1955.

7. He survived the electric chair

Official Court Records, St Martin Parish, St Martinville (Suit no. 2161, 12–14 September 1945).

Newspapers: *The Weekly Messenger* (St Martinville, La.), 10 November 1944; 14 September 1945; 3 May–14 June and 15 November 1946; 17 January and 25 April–9 May 1947. *The Times-Picayune* (New Orleans), 11 November 1944. *The New York Times*, 16 May 1946; 4–5 and 11–12 June 1946; 19 November 1946; 14–15 and 30 January 1947; 11 February 1947; 19 and 23 April 1947; 1 May 1947; 6–10 May 1947. *The Times* (London), 14 January and 10 May 1947.

SETTINGS FOR SLAUGHTER

Douglas Wynn

An isolated farmhouse . . . the woodland area known as
Cannock Chase . . . the close-knit community of a Welsh
mining town . . . these are some of the places where
hideous murders have been committed, and where the
location has played an important role in the crime.
Whether a remote spot provides the perfect place to
dispose of a body, or a weapon, or whether local feeling
about the police hampers a criminal investigation, the
setting for slaughter can influence the act of murder as
well as what happens afterwards.

Some of our most macabre murders are reconstructed in
this spine-tingling collection drawn from all over the
British Isles.

FUTURA PUBLICATIONS
NON-FICTION/TRUE CRIME
0 7088 4366 2

ALONE WITH THE DEVIL

Ronald Markman and Dominick Bosco

Dr Ronald Markman has one of the most frightening jobs in the world. He is a forensic psychiatrist – someone who by his profession regularly finds himself alone in a room with a devilish killer, someone whose courtroom testimony will provide vital evidence as to whether the murderer is sane or insane – whether or not he is legally responsible for his hideous deeds.

Alone with the Devil is Markman's riveting analysis of some of his toughest cases – two of Charles Manson's followers who went on a murderous crusade through California; the infamous 'Vampire of Sacramento' whose insatiable thirst for blood drove him into a horrific butchering rage; and many other notorious, twisted killers whose crimes have included cannibalism, torture and slow death.

Fascinating and terrifying, a dark odyssey through psychopathic minds – *Alone with the Devil* is true-crime analysis at its best.

'An educative, horrifying book'
Booklist

'Chilling . . . by turns horrifying, fascinating'
Kirkus Reviews

'Engrossing if disquieting study'
Publishers Weekly

FUTURA PUBLICATIONS
NON-FICTION/TRUE CRIME
0 7088 4848 6

GHOST HUNTERS
True Stories from the World's Most Famous Demonologists

Ed and Lorraine Warren
with
Robert David Chase

In over three thousand investigations in the last forty years, Ed and Lorraine Warren have been helping people to understand, cope with and overcome terrifying experiences from the supernatural. Here, some of their incredible encounters are detailed:

– A 16-year-old girl suffers repeated sexual attacks from one of the most feared types of demons, the incubus.

– The entire population of a village is driven from its homes by satanic forces.

– Frequent sightings of the legendary Bigfoot are reported by an impoverished hillside community.

– In a psychic vision, three men are identified as the murderers of a beautiful young woman.

GHOST HUNTERS offers concrete proof that the demonic underworld exists and is much closer to home than most of us realize. This collection of baffling and bloodcurdling cases will have you sleeping with the lights on.

"These down-to-earth and otherworldly snippets of 'demonic infestation' will interest ghost watchers everywhere"
Booklist

FUTURA PUBLICATIONS
NON-FICTION
0 7088 4837 0

WOULD YOU BELIEVE IT?
Odd Tales from a Weird World

Philip Mason

MADNESS, MARVELS AND MIRACLES . . .

Enter a freakish world of horror and humour in stories so perverse, so macabre, so madly improbable that no fiction writer would dare present them . . .

● In January 1984, Ainsley Huskisson wrote The Lord's Prayer four times on the back of a 12½p stamp.

● Jailed for seven years for polygamy, Indonesian Ali Nasution's plea for mitigation rested on the fact that he had already divorced 93 of his 121 wives.

● 28-year-old Asif Mohammed from Dundee, suffering from depression in November 1984, chopped both his feet off. Surgeons later sewed them back on.

● A 14-stone Californian woman was acquitted by a San José court in March 1983 of killing her son. She had sat on him for two hours as a punishment.

WOULD YOU BELIEVE IT?

These breathtaking, mindboggling, stomach-turning facts are guaranteed to hold you spellbound. Now read on . . . the world out there is even stranger than your wildest imaginings . . .

FUTURA PUBLICATIONS
NON-FICTION
0 7088 4780 3

DR CRIPPEN'S DIARY

Emlyn Williams

Neither novel nor biography, DR CRIPPEN'S DIARY is a dramatic mixture of true crime and inventive fiction, by the bestselling author of BEYOND BELIEF.

Interpreting known facts through his knowledge of criminal psychology, Emlyn Williams has created the journal Crippen *could* have kept, from his twenty-first birthday to his last hours. Following the fate of his monstrous wife and his young lover, Ethel Le Neve, it brings to life one of the most notorious murderers of the twentieth century.

Ingenious and convincing, Crippen – seen for decades as a vicious murderer – emerges as a tragically misunderstood character, tried beyond endurance.

FUTURA PUBLICATIONS
CRIME/FICTION
0 7088 3929 0

HELL RANCH

Clifford L. Linedecker

In early 1989, American pre-med student Mark Kilroy
mysteriously vanished during a night out in Matamoros,
Mexico. Even those who feared for his life never
imagined the horror that awaited him.

A month later, Mark's mutilated grisly remains were
found at the remote Santa Elena Ranch, just outside
Metamoros. And within a few days, the horrifically
dismembered bodies of fourteen other men and boys were
recovered there by U.S. and Mexican police officers.
They had been hacked to death, shot, hanged and
tortured.

The investigation into the gruesome murders at Santa
Elena Ranch would lead to the discovery of a bizarre
demonic blood cult, whose members were ruthless drug
dealers and satanists. This is the true, penetrating story of
the cult's inhuman, atrocious crimes and the eventual
capture and arrest of the murderers of HELL RANCH.

FUTURA PUBLICATIONS
NON-FICTION/TRUE CRIME
0 7088 4760 9

WAINWRIGHT'S BEAT
One Man's Journey with a Police Force

John Wainwright

'a fascinating autobiography'
Evening Standard

John Wainwright joined the West Riding of Yorkshire constabulary on 8 September 1947 'to get a house'. It was to be twenty years before he finally handed in his uniform.

In this fascinating memoir of his time in the force, the highly successful crime novelist describes with candour and warmth the life of an ordinary copper on the beat, from rescuing dogs to murder hunts. The pleasure, the pain, the joy and the sheer frustration of being a guardian of the peace is vividly recounted, including the episode when Wainwright is ordered by his commanding officer to commit perjury. His refusal to do so meant he was never promoted in twenty years of service.

'a host of revealing tales'
Guardian

'a shrewd, perceptive view of police life as it was and largely still is' John Stalker, Ex-Deputy Chief Constable of the Manchester Police

FUTURA PUBLICATIONS
NON-FICTION/AUTOBIOGRAPHY
0 7088 4199 6

OBSESSION

Ramsey Campbell

THEY HAD UNLEASHED A DEMONIC POWER BEYOND THEIR CONTROL . . .

Four kids burn with adolescent frustration in a dead-end seaside town. In a bid to change their mundane lives, they form a secret, unearthly pact, each one calling on the powers of a dark supernatural force with a wish to be fulfilled. But what begins as an innocent game soon becomes a chilling nightmare. Their desires are granted, but for a horrifying price . . .

'The kind of novel that would be up for literary prizes if anyone bothered to look beyond the genre labels'
City Limits

'An ingenious, beautifully crafted tale . . . Campbell writes of our deepest fears in a precise, clear prose that manages to be beautiful and terrifying at the same time'
Washington Post

'The undisputed master of the psychological horror novel'
ROBERT HOLDSTOCK

'One of the finest exponents of the classic British ghost story' *Daily Telegraph*

'Campbell does more than jar the nerves and chill the spine: he assails one's very grip on reality'
Publishers Weekly

FUTURA PUBLICATIONS
FICTION/HORROR
0 7088 4396 4

What horrifying secret lies within . . .

THE VIOLET CLOSET

Gary Gottesfeld

A terrified young voice cries out from the dark.

"Da hurt . . . Da kill . . . Help me!"

These are the panic-stricken words of a little girl phoning in to Dr Rena Halbrook's radio show. But who is little Alice – and where is she?

As Charles Halleran, veteran reporter, hears the child's plea over his car radio, he recalls another little girl named Alice who died in New York 18 years before. Can there possibly be a connection?

As the anniversary of that shocking death approaches, Charles teams up with Rena in a desperate search to uncover dark secrets from the past and prevent almost certain tragedy from striking again.

Their race against time will lead them on a spine-tingling chase from the placid streets of Beverly Hills to the burnt-out tenements of the South Bronx. And the more they discover, the surer they become that what they still don't know could definitely hurt them . . .

FUTURA PUBLICATIONS
FICTION
0 7088 4540 1

All Futura Books are available at your bookshop or newsagent, or can be ordered from the following address:

Futura Books,
Cash Sales Department,
P.O. Box 11,
Falmouth,
Cornwall TR10 9EN.

Alternatively you may fax your order to the above address. Fax No. 0326 76423.

Payments can be made as follows: Cheque, postal order (payable to Macdonald & Co (Publishers) Ltd) or by credit cards, Visa/Access. Do not send cash or currency. UK customers: please send a cheque or postal order (no currency) and allow 80p for postage and packing for the first book plus 20p for each additional book up to a maximum charge of £2.00.

B.F.P.O. customers please allow 80p for the first book plus 20p for each additional book.

Overseas customers including Ireland, please allow £1.50 for postage and packing for the first book, £1.00 for the second book, and 30p for each additional book.

NAME (Block Letters) ....

ADDRESS ....

....

☐ I enclose my remittance for _____

☐ I wish to pay by Access/Visa Card

Number ☐☐☐☐ ☐☐☐☐ ☐☐☐☐ ☐☐☐☐ ☐☐☐☐

Card Expiry Date ☐☐☐☐